CHOOSE STRONG

3-MINUTE
DEVOTIONS
FOR TEEN GUYS

CHOOSE STRONG

3-MINUTE DEVOTIONS
FOR TEEN GUYS

ELIJAH ADKINS

BARBOUR
PUBLISHING

ISBN 978-1-63609-851-7

Published by Barbour Publishing, Inc., 1810 Barbour Drive, Uhrichsville, Ohio 44683, www.barbourbooks.com

Our mission is to inspire the world with the life-changing message of the Bible.

Member of the
Evangelical Christian
Publishers Association

Printed in China.

CHOOSE STRONG

These devotions were written especially for guys like you, guys who have important choices to make in life—either God's way or the world's way, right or wrong, strong or weak. . . . This book will help you to choose wisely.

In just three minutes, you'll be well on your way to the good life—the *strength-filled* life—God intended for you.

Minute 1: Read the day's Bible verse and reflect on what God's Word is saying.

Minute 2: Read the devotional and think about what it means for your life.

Minute 3: Pray and grow closer to God.

Turn the page and discover how three minutes of quiet time with God can change your life!

A TALL ORDER

Be ye holy; for I am holy.

1 PETER 1:16 KJV

Yikes, you may be thinking, *today's verse sounds like a tall order!* Holiness is something that only God naturally possesses, so why would He expect us to follow suit? Isn't this an impossible task?

Yes. We definitely can't do it on our own. But when we choose to surrender ourselves to God's grace—when we choose His strength—our unrighteousness is replaced by His holiness. And He doesn't only clean our slate and erase our sins; He also gives us the strength to work toward this impossible goal. Of course our actions will never catch up to our status, but the longer we serve God, the closer we'll get.

Holiness may be a tall order, but God will help you rise to His calling on your life.

. . . .

Thank You, Lord, for giving me standing that I could never earn on my own. Your holiness is my goal, so help me never to stop working toward it.

KEEP LOOKING

Seek the LORD and his strength;
seek his presence continually!
1 CHRONICLES 16:11 ESV

If you've ever watched strong people train at the gym, you know that the key to pumping up your muscles really boils down to one word: *intentionality.*

As any bodybuilder will tell you, strength isn't something that just happens out of the blue. No, it takes setting a clear, achievable goal and working tirelessly until that goal is reached. . .and then setting a new goal and starting the process all over again.

Spiritual strength is no different. If you want to improve your walk with God—whether it's by boosting your faith, getting more courage, or powering up your prayer life—you'll never get there by just wishing it will happen. You must "hit the gym" each day, praying and studying God's Word even when you don't feel like it.

God's strength is always there—you just have to look for it.

God, give me the endurance to
keep seeking Your strength.

STAYING THE COURSE

*Finally, be strong in the Lord and
in the strength of his might.*
EPHESIANS 6:10 ESV

Have you ever pulled an all-nighter to study for a test? If so, you know how difficult it can be to resist the overwhelming urge to sleep.

The Christian life can feel like this sometimes. You will have days when you don't think you can continue—when the problems at home are overwhelming, when your friends turn their backs on you, when you're mocked at school for your faith, when your peers try convincing you to do wrong things. Staying strong may take everything you have and then some.

However, today's verse says that during these times, giving up isn't an option. Even when your mind tries to convince you to embrace weakness, God will give you the ability to choose His strength instead. Giving in may feel good for a moment, but staying the course will have eternal rewards.

. . . .

*Lord, hold my attention steady—on You—when
life is hard. Help me stay the course.*

POWER SOURCE

He gives power to the weak and
strength to the powerless.
ISAIAH 40:29 NLT

Choosing strength means choosing God.

Left to our own devices, we become burned out—fogged-up, sin-encrusted flashlights with dead batteries. But *with God*—well, that's a different story. Suddenly that lifeless bulb becomes a floodlight, streaking a beam of hope and righteousness across the darkness of our lives.

How do you connect to this unlimited power source? It's simple! By entrusting your life to the one who can make you shine. By rejecting self-reliance in favor of total submission. By seeking strength in an all-powerful God. No longer will you have to struggle with feelings of inadequacy in the face of powerful temptation—God will give you all the strength you need to resist.

. . . .

Father, thank You for being my ultimate power source.
Help me always to look to You for the strength I need.

THAT'S AN ORDER!

Have not I commanded thee?
Be strong and of a good courage.
JOSHUA 1:9 KJV

Imagine walking into your first day of boot camp. As you stand in line with other soon-to-be soldiers, Sarge gives his first order: "All right, everyone—fifty push-ups!" Everyone—except you—drops immediately to the ground. "Eh, I don't feel like it," you say. "Can we do something easier?" Sarge nods his head and says, "Okay, maybe I was a bit harsh. Do whatever makes you feel comfortable."

Yeah, right.

Laziness, no matter what form it takes, just won't fly in boot camp, and it won't fly in the Christian walk either. God has *commanded*—not suggested—that we choose strength when the going gets tough and fear threatens to crush our resolve. But unlike Sarge, God won't just stand there and watch you sweat; instead, He'll be on the ground beside you, giving you the strength you need to lift yourself up again.

. . . .

God, give me the willpower to choose
Your strength over my weakness.

THE BEST DEFENSE

The LORD is my strength and my shield.
PSALM 28:7 KJV

You should know that every morning when you get out of bed, the devil has plans. He'll use anything from a stubbed toe to a bully's insults to try dragging you down. And if you don't have God's strength, your defenses will be about as effective as standing on a battlefield wearing nothing but a T-shirt and jeans. Soon those fiery arrows will hit their mark, making you feel like the devil's pincushion.

But if you trust in God's strength, you have a protection so strong that it makes Captain America's shield look like rotten tree bark. But wait! Before God's shield can protect you, you have to do one thing: *take it with you.* God's strength, as powerful as it is, is still a choice you must make.

Are you willing to pick up His shield today?

. . . .

Lord, thank You for protecting me from
Satan's plans. Help me surround myself
with the power of Your Word.

NEVER GONNA LET YOU DOWN

*"Be strong. . .because GOD, your God,
is striding ahead of you. He's right there with you.
He won't let you down; he won't leave you."*
DEUTERONOMY 31:6 MSG

Odds are you know how it feels to be let down by
someone you once trusted or admired. Maybe it was
a parent, a friend, a role model, or a celebrity. Even if
this person's betrayal was entirely unintentional, it still
stung—and it still broke your trust.

Today's verse assures that God will *never* let you
down. When you have doubts about the future—when
you wonder if your dedication will ever pay off—you
can rest assured, knowing that it's impossible for God
to break His promises. If He says He'll be with you, then
He'll be with you—full stop. His strength isn't a "maybe"
or a "we'll see." As long as you're trusting in Him, it's a
rock-solid guarantee.

You can bet your life on it!

. . . .

Lord, help me fully trust Your promise never to leave.

INFINITE STRENGTH

My flesh and my heart may fail,
but God is the strength of my heart.
PSALM 73:26 NASB

Inside the heart of every teen is a metaphorical bucket that we can call "strength storage." When life gets hard and problems multiply, the strength storage runs dangerously low. The heart starts sputtering and alarms start blaring to the tune of fatigue and frustration. Pretty soon the bucket is empty, and what happens next depends entirely on a teen's relationship with God.

For the teen who doesn't have a personal relationship with Christ, full panic ensues, followed by a bout of severe depression that may or may not go away. But for the Christian, something amazing happens: this bucket gets pushed to the side and replaced by another bucket—one that *never* runs dry.

This renewed strength comes straight from God— the only source of infinite power. So today, don't worry if your strength is running low: God has a bottomless supply always on hand.

. . . .

Lord, help me never rely on my own limited power.
Fuel my soul instead with Your infinite strength.

THE END

God in dependable love shows up on
time, shows me my enemies in ruin.
PSALM 59:10 MSG

Have you ever read a suspense novel filled with danger and edge-of-your-seat action? If so, you probably know how tempting it is to peek at the final chapter. But you refuse, knowing the whole story would be ruined if you skipped to the end.

However, real life is a bit different. When all the wrong people seem to be winning, we want to look ahead, but the cold, solid barrier of time blocks our sight. The only one who is able to see the future is God—and He has mercifully given us a glimpse of it in His Word. When we flip to the back of our Bibles, we find a truth that can strengthen even the weakest of believers: we win!

Even if you don't know the details of how God will conquer evil, just know that He will. Then sit back and enjoy the ride.

. . . .

Lord, thank You for assuring us of evil's final defeat.

WEAKLING NO MORE

*When we were yet without strength,
in due time Christ died for the ungodly.*
ROMANS 5:6 KJV

Today's verse is the spiritual equivalent of a before-and-after image. Before a person knows God, his soul is scrawny and malnourished, crumpling under the lightest touch from the enemy. But as soon as God's love enters his heart, the strengthening process begins. The fruit of the Spirit starts replacing his weaknesses, and the whirlpool of temptation begins to lose its pull.

In short, he's not a weakling anymore.

Maybe this describes your journey so far. Or maybe you're just starting out, eager to discover how strong God will make you. Either way, don't give up! Living the Christian life is like trying to count to infinity—even though you'll never reach perfection in this life, you'll always be one step above where you were yesterday.

That's what it means to choose strength!

. . . .

*Father God, thank You for fueling my
spiritual progress. Help me continue growing
stronger and rising toward You.*

GREATNESS

Let us not grow weary of doing good.

GALATIANS 6:9 ESV

"Greatness is a lot of small things done well." Maybe you've heard this quote by the famous Christian football player Ray Lewis, but do you know what it really means? On the surface, it sounds so noble yet simple. *Just keep doing the right thing. Hang in there.*

The truth is, there's nothing easy or glamorous about it. Greatness means refusing the drink even when your friends belittle you for it. Greatness means choosing to attend church on Sunday morning even when your body craves another hour of sleep. Greatness is taking the trash out when no one asks. Greatness is doing the very thing you *don't* want to do in the moment. Why? Because you know it's what God wants; and what God wants overrides what you want.

Today, don't choose the easy path over the right one. Instead, choose to be strong. Choose to follow God. Choose greatness.

. . . .

Lord, please give me the strength to
replace my wants with Your plan.

ALWAYS WATCHING

*The eyes of the LORD run to and fro throughout the
whole earth, to shew himself strong in the behalf
of them whose heart is perfect toward him.*

2 CHRONICLES 16:9 KJV

The first part of today's verse may sound like God is
an overbearing dictator, always watching for us to slip
up. But look closely at the rest of the sentence. God
is not watching for us to make mistakes. He's watching
for ways in which He can work through us!

God, of course, can work through anyone He wants,
but He is especially looking for those with pure hearts.
Why? So He can strengthen those people and display
His power to the world.

Today, remember that each choice you make, no
matter how small, is a choice that determines the path
of your heart—and whether you'll receive God's strength.
Are you ready for Him to use you?

. . . .

*Lord, may my heart be perfect toward You so
I can be a willing vessel of Your power.*

HUTS AND TOWERS

The name of the LORD is a strong tower;
the righteous man runs into it and is safe.
PROVERBS 18:10 ESV

Picture this: You're on a battlefield, surrounded by whizzing bullets and cracking mortar shells. Most of your comrades have fallen, and the enemy is only a hundred yards away. To your left is an old hut with two walls still standing, and to your right, a stone fortress that's actively being guarded by soldiers who serve your side.

If you had to make a break for one of these locations, which would you choose?

Judging by the way many people live their lives, most would apparently choose the old hut. Rather than putting their trust in God—a strong, impenetrable fortress—they place their hope in things that can never protect, things like money, fame, and power.

When faced with a choice, don't run to something that will be destroyed; instead, place your trust in the strong name of the Lord.

. . . .

Lord, whenever I'm faced with a choice between
You and the world, help me always to choose You.

CLIFFHANGER

"You must love the LORD your God with all your heart, all your soul, all your mind, and all your strength."
MARK 12:30 NLT

Imagine dangling over the edge of a cliff, holding tightly to a rock jutting outward from the side of the chasm. In that moment, do you think to yourself, *This rock is a bit uncomfortable, so I'll just loosen my grip a bit*? Of course not!

So why do many Christians act this way toward God? God is our sole salvation—our life-saving rock. If we truly grasp the nature of our relationship with Him, our tight grip will come naturally, just like gripping that ledge comes naturally to one who is hanging over the cliff. The moment we start ignoring God and pushing Him out of our lives, however, is the moment that letting go becomes easier and easier.

So don't let it come to that. Don't allow weakness to loosen your grip. Keep choosing God's strength.

. . . .

*God, help me continue loving You
with all of me—not just part.*

STRONG ENOUGH

He said unto me, My grace is sufficient for thee:
for my strength is made perfect in weakness.

2 CORINTHIANS 12:9 KJV

God wants us to hold on to Him with all our strength, but what happens when "all our strength" amounts to nothing but weakness? In our moment of utter helplessness, will God let us fall?

No! Today's verse says that when we're at our weakest point—when we have no strength remaining—that's when God's strength takes over, proving His power to anyone watching. Right before you lose your grip, He grabs you, giving you just enough traction to keep holding on.

The truth is, none of us can hold on by ourselves—the gravity of our fallen human nature is just too powerful. But thanks to God's strength that fills the gap of our weakness, we'll never have to stress over our lack of power.

When we're weak, God is strong.

. . . .

Thank You, God, for being
stronger than my weakness.

DUELING SPIRITS

God hath not given us the spirit of fear; but of power, and of love, and of a sound mind.

2 TIMOTHY 1:7 KJV

Out of the four emotions in today's verse, which one sounds most appealing to you? Chances are, your answer is a three-way tie and it *doesn't* include fear.

When unbridled fear starts seeping into your mind, it immediately begins fighting against the mindset that God wants you to have. Your body becomes a battleground between dueling spirits—a smiling exterior filled with anguish and conflict.

But there's good news: you get to choose the outcome! God hasn't left you powerless—He has given you the ability to pick a side and fight on its behalf. If you choose fear, then fear is the side that wins. Choosing God's power, love, and peace, however, ensures the triumph of a strong and godly spirit.

Which will you choose today?

. . . .

Father, help me choose Your Spirit over the harmful spirits that are trying to enter my mind.

DESPERATELY WICKED

The heart is deceitful above all things, and
desperately wicked: who can know it?
JEREMIAH 17:9 KJV

Perhaps one of the most striking developments in modern psychology is the discovery that the human mind looks a lot like what's described in the Bible—desperately wicked. Each human, even the "best" among us, is capable of unspeakable evil. Our worst instincts lie just below the surface of our consciousness, ready to spring to the forefront at the slightest hint of distress or inconvenience.

That's why God's strength is so necessary. On our own, we're little more than "whitewashed tombs" (Matthew 23:27 ESV)—clean-looking exteriors hiding a multitude of sins. But with His help, the darkest parts of our psyche begin not just to diminish but to wither and die, killed by the holy light of God's love.

Each one of us has a sickness in the heart—will you say yes to the cure?

. . . .

Thank You, Jesus, for offering a cure
for my spiritual heart disease.

SIMPLY CHOOSE

Submit yourselves therefore to God.
Resist the devil, and he will flee from you.
JAMES 4:7 ESV

Let's face it: being a Christian teen in today's world isn't easy. Whether it's the pull of peer pressure, the allure of pornography, or the false freedom of popularity, there are about as many temptations surrounding you as there are seconds in the day.

But before you collapse in despair, today's verse delivers some very good news: all you must do is *choose.* That's right—God knows how impossible it would be for you to resist every temptation, so He grants power to you whenever you choose to resist. In that moment, your strength is not your own—it comes straight from above, and it's powerful enough to send Satan packing.

So today, don't waffle between choosing God or choosing Satan. Pick God's side, and He'll give you the power to win the war.

. . . .

Thank You, God, for the supernatural strength
You've given me. Help me to choose that strength
each time weakness threatens to take over.

TRUE STRENGTH

To sum up, all of you be harmonious,
sympathetic, loving, compassionate, and
humble; not returning evil for evil or insult
for insult, but giving a blessing instead.
1 PETER 3:8–9 NASB

When most people think of strength, they think of historical figures like Alexander the Great, dressed in impenetrable armor and ready to demonstrate physical dominance over their enemies. But when it comes to God's children, true strength is just the opposite: it flows from humility—a desire to serve rather than conquer.

True strength is closing your mouth when offensive insults are hurled your way. True strength is picking up some dropped textbooks for the guy who shoved you yesterday. True strength is praying for God to give you a caring heart when hatred is all you feel. True strength is kindness. True strength is compassion. True strength is love.

. . . .

Lord, help me choose true strength today—
not the false strength that's defined by the
world. Your strength will be the only thing left
once everything else has passed away.

THE WINNING SIDE

*"Those who are victorious will sit with me
on my throne, just as I was victorious and
sat with my Father on his throne."*

REVELATION 3:21 NLT

Today's verse promises something amazing: those who are victorious through Christ will get a seat at the throne of Jesus! They will one day stand triumphantly over the forces of evil that tried to drag them down. What a wonderful promise!

But it gets even better: God doesn't leave us on our own to fight the devil; in fact, He fights *for* us (Exodus 14:14). No mortal really wins over sin—but we can always choose the winning side and let God compensate for our weakness. And, after our battle is over, God rewards our choice with a celebration we don't really deserve.

Will you choose the winning side today?

. . . .

*Lord God, thank You for guaranteeing victory
for the person who trusts in You. Help me
to always choose the winning side.*

FINISH WHAT HE'S STARTED

I am certain that God, who began the good work
within you, will continue his work until it is finally
finished on the day when Christ Jesus returns.

PHILIPPIANS 1:6 NLT

Do you struggle with finishing what you've started? Maybe you pursue a brand-new hobby every few weeks, jumping from goal to goal but never fully arriving. If so, it might be hard to imagine yourself reaching the end of your life with your salvation intact. What if your spiritual dedication is just as short-lived as everything else?

Today's verse is here to assure you otherwise. If you have the desire to serve God—as long as you're making that choice—God will preserve your soul, no matter how burned out you feel. All you have to do is *keep choosing*. That alone takes strength, but guess what? God will give you strength for that too!

. . . .

Lord, give me the strength to keep choosing Your
love whenever I'm tempted to quit. Thank You
for promising to finish what You've started.

SACRIFICE

I urge you, brothers and sisters, by the mercies of God, to present your bodies as a living and holy sacrifice, acceptable to God, which is your spiritual service of worship.

ROMANS 12:1 NASB

It takes a lot of strength to offer up your life to God, but that's exactly what He asks of us. The Christian life isn't a hobby—it's a life-changing choice that impacts every aspect of your existence. It's the act of handing over your most prized possessions to God, trusting that He is most qualified to handle them. That's why today's verse calls this action a *sacrifice*.

But there's good news: Jesus has already done all the hard work. By sacrificing not just His desires but His life, He serves as our example, strengthening us in our moments of weakness. Jesus understands how hard sacrifice is, but He also understands just how amazing the rewards are on the other side.

. . . .

Lord Jesus, give me the strength to lay down everything—even my life—in service to You.

WORTH FIGHTING FOR

Strive for peace with everyone.
HEBREWS 12:14 ESV

Are you ever bogged down by never-ending arguments with your family and friends? If so, you're not alone. Today's verse makes it clear that peace isn't our natural state—it's something we must "strive" for.

The Bible repeatedly calls us to go to combat with our warring instincts—to kill our desire for violence and squash our need for superiority. In fact, the only way to live out the Christian life is to be at peace with those who disagree with you. Why? Because our real enemies aren't flesh and blood but rather spiritual forces that take a lot more than an angry voice to defeat them (Ephesians 6:12). Once you start down God's path, you'll realize that a turned cheek is far more powerful than a raised fist (Matthew 5:39).

Peace, as God's Word proclaims, is truly worth fighting for.

. . . .

Almighty God, I need Your strength to stay peaceful. Please help replace my defensiveness with the peace of Your love.

TREASURE HUNT

Look for good and not sin, that you may live.
AMOS 5:14 NLV

Imagine this: a friend gives you a map that points the way to buried treasure. This search, according to the map, will take you through rainforests and deserts, around quicksand, and into deadly caves.

Before you begin, you ask your friend, "By the way, what's the treasure?"

"Just trash," your friend says. "Still want to go?"

The smart thing to do would be to rip up the map and walk away, but many people jump right into this kind of worthless treasure hunt, devoting their lives to nothing more than a pile of trash. Many people spend years chasing things that will never satisfy, ignoring the true treasure map of God's Word.

Remember that real strength lies not in the search, but in the thing you're searching for. It's what sets apart courage from foolishness—noble dedication from a pointless waste of time.

What kind of treasure are you seeking today?

. . . .

God, direct me toward Your worthwhile treasure and keep me from pointless pursuits.

HOLY AGREEMENT

*"I have made an agreement with my eyes not
to look with desire at a young woman."*
JOB 31:1 NLV

If you're working hard to live a godly life, today's verse
may seem disheartening. Advertisements, social media
accounts, websites, video games, book covers—basically
every visual media seem to conspire to promote lust.

That's why making an "agreement" with your eyes
is so important. Accidentally seeing an unholy image
isn't a sin; but, like everything else, it all comes down
to choice. Will you choose to avert your eyes to avoid
walking into a situation that might exploit your weaknesses, or will you choose to linger on the sight, letting
it corrupt your mind and chip away at your willpower
to resist the next temptation that comes along?

Today, make a holy agreement with your eyes. If
you're truly serious about your promise, God will help
you honor it.

*Lord, strengthen my eyes, giving them the
ability to pull away from harmful images.*

REFINING FIRE

You have put us to the test, God;
You have refined us as silver is refined.
PSALM 66:10 NASB

When it comes to our spiritual growth, God is not messing around. He is willing to use anything—even temporarily painful situations—to bring us closer to a fulfilling walk with Him.

C. S. Lewis summed it up nicely in *A Grief Observed* when he said, "What do people mean when they say, 'I am not afraid of God because I know He is good'? Have they never even been to a dentist?" Those who say God would never make us uncomfortable clearly haven't gotten the Bible's message. Life is ugly sometimes, but it's not our duty as Christians to make the pain go away; rather, it's our duty to choose strength through the pain. That way, even when the suffering lessens, our character will be stronger than ever.

. . . .

God, strengthen me so that I'll be able to face
whatever fires may come. I want life's hard
times to purify rather than weaken my soul.

ANSWER KEY

Thy word have I hid in mine heart,
that I might not sin against thee.
PSALM 119:11 KJV

When you're faced with a difficult exam at school, what do you do? Do you forget about it until test day, trusting your instincts to carry you through? Or do you crack open your textbooks and start memorizing?

Hopefully, you choose the latter! Memorization is the most effective way to pass tests—even the spiritual types. Yes, the Christian life is like a class—and temptations are the pop quizzes. That's why continuous Bible study is important: it shifts the weight off your own flawed intuition and onto the infinitely powerful truth of God's Word. No longer do you have to "trust your gut"—you have access to a much more reliable source of information.

Today, get in the habit of memorizing small chunks of the Bible at a time. It's the answer key for all of life's questions!

Lord, thank You for giving us all the
answers we need to live for You.

STRENGTH LINE

Watch and pray, that ye enter not into temptation:
the spirit indeed is willing, but the flesh is weak.
MATTHEW 26:41 KJV

Trying to live the Christian life without prayer is like trying to win a marathon without training. You might last a mile or two before you collapse in exhaustion, vowing never to do that again.

Why? Because our bodies just aren't capable of resisting life's temptations on their own. Sure, we can choose to do the right thing when it's relatively easy, but the moment push comes to shove, it's human nature to cave in. Prayer, however, opens a line of strength between us and God. Why else do you think Jesus prayed constantly, especially as His crucifixion drew near? He knew He needed all the strength He could get while He was in His earthly body, so He wasted no opportunity to ask His Father to provide it.

How healthy is your "strength line" today?

. . . .

Lord, remind me to pray at all times—good and bad.

HUNGER

Jesus. . .was led by the Spirit in the
wilderness for forty days, being tempted by the
devil. And he ate nothing during those days.
And when they were ended, he was hungry.

LUKE 4:1–2 ESV

You'd think going forty days without food would weaken any man, even the Son of God, to the point of giving in to even the slightest temptation. But after this passage, Jesus faced not one but *three* temptations from the master of temptation himself, and He passed each one.

Even though Jesus' body was weak to the point of death, His spirit was just as healthy and well fed as ever. Why? Because Jesus kept His line of communication with His Father wide open, continuously allowing spiritual strength to flow from heaven to earth. That way the state of His body had no sway over the state of His spirit. His hunger for food may have been strong, but His hunger for God proved stronger.

. . . .

Lord God, help me never stop praying to You—
You're my sole source of spiritual strength.

BAD COMPANY

*Do not be deceived: "Bad company
corrupts good morals."*
1 CORINTHIANS 15:33 NASB

As a teen, you're probably surrounded by people whom Paul might call "bad company." Whether they're from school, across the street, or even in your church, bad influences are everywhere these days, trying their best to corrupt godly minds.

So what's a Christian teen to do? Shut himself off from everyone and never go outside? No, the Bible speaks against that too (1 Corinthians 5:9-10). Rather, today's verse teaches that Christians should seek out good company instead of choosing to spend time with the bad. Hounded by a friend who keeps trying to offer you drugs or alcohol? Don't be afraid to walk away. Bothered by the immorality flowing from that television show? Just reach for the remote. It's in these small moments of decision that true strength is built.

Whose company are you in today?

. . . .

*Lord, make me wiser in my choice of
company. Help me seek out godly
influences instead of corrupting ones.*

SPIRIT VS. FLESH

*But I say, walk by the Spirit, and you will
not gratify the desires of the flesh.*
GALATIANS 5:16 ESV

Who would you say is your worst enemy? That bully
at school? No. That friend who criticizes your faith?
Still no.

Believe it or not, your worst enemy is. . .yourself.
More specifically, it's your sinful nature—the part of you
that screams *yes* when your mind, heart, and soul know
to resist. The Bible calls this aspect of you the "flesh,"
and today's verse offers a way to beat it once and for all.

Walking in the Spirit (studying the Bible, praying,
and striving to live in God's will) ensures that your fleshly
desires will have no place in your heart. You may still
feel them from time to time, but they'll be little more
than remains of the past.

In short, there will be no room for weakness when
strength is your new mode of operation!

. . . .

*Lord, help me walk in Your Spirit, building
up the strength to triumph over my flesh.*

IMPENETRABLE

Put on the whole armor of God, that you may be able to stand against the schemes of the devil.
 EPHESIANS 6:11 ESV

When you're in the middle of an all-out war with the devil—when fiery arrows of temptations are blazing by and javelins of doubt are raining down—your own strength doesn't matter as much as the strength of the armor that protects you. A single gap might prove lethal. That's why today's verse stresses the importance of having a full set—the "whole armor of God."

When you have the helmet of salvation (6:17), the devil's cruel whispers can't penetrate your mind. When you swing the sword of the Spirit (6:17), the charging sins of your past fall lifeless to the ground. When you wield the shield of faith (6:16), doubts bounce off like hailstones on solid steel. In short, cultivating a closer walk with God means clothing yourself in His attributes.

How's your armor holding up today?

. . . .

Thank You, God, for offering me armor in the heat of battle. Help me never to take it off.

RUN

Now flee from youthful lusts and pursue
righteousness, faith, love, and peace with those
who call on the Lord from a pure heart.

2 TIMOTHY 2:22 NASB

In today's culture, it's practically a crime to deny your-self worldly pleasures. Rather than encouraging your desire to live in God's will, culture disguises spiritual weakness with deceitful buzz words like "self-empowerment" and "liberation" and then pummels you with them until you give in.

Sometimes when these voices have you pinned to a wall and your willpower is running on empty, the strongest thing you can do is *run*—flee to God's Word for a much-needed dose of strength and truth.

God doesn't call us to be cowards, but He also doesn't call us to fight unnecessary battles. When you're down and out of strength, His Word can be your refuge.

. . . .

Father, give me the wisdom to fight when
I need to fight and run when I need to run.
Teach me how to take shelter in Your Word.

CHEAP VICTORY

*Beloved, never avenge yourselves, but leave
it to the wrath of God, for it is written,
"Vengeance is mine, I will repay, says the Lord."*
ROMANS 12:19 ESV

If there's one lesson God wants us to learn about our interactions with others, it's this: strength does not equal power.

Suppose you're presented with a golden opportunity to humiliate that guy who pokes fun at you all the time. Maybe you've learned an embarrassing secret about his past, and you have the evidence to prove it. In that moment, which is the "stronger" option—to spill the secret and get sweet revenge or stay silent and pray for him instead?

You know the answer. The fact that you can easily do something cruel doesn't make you strong—it's your willingness to do the hard thing that proves your strength. Why? Because the toughest battles aren't won with words and fists; they're won with humility and love.

. . . .

*God, help me choose strength over power,
integrity over a cheap victory.*

SOLD ON TRUTH

Beloved, do not believe every spirit, but test the spirits to see whether they are from God, for many false prophets have gone out into the world.

1 JOHN 4:1 ESV

Wouldn't life be so much simpler if you could just lean back and believe everything you hear? No longer would you have to try finding the truth. You could just accept what you're told, no questions asked. Don't worry: every scam artist, telemarketer, palm reader, and car salesman on earth would support your newfound naïveté. You'd be in safe hands!

Obviously, this is sarcasm.

Not only are there people who prey on ignorance and misplaced trust; there is also a plethora of ideas about God's identity all vying for your attention. Only one is correct, however, and today's verse tells us to always make sure we know which one that is.

Today, don't be sold on a lie—stay sold on God's truth instead!

. . . .

Lord, give me a discerning heart. I never want to be led astray by smooth words and empty promises.

WHIRLPOOL

*Do not remember the sins of my
youth or my wrongdoings.*

Psalm 25:7 NASB

If you didn't get to know God until recently, your past may feel like a whirlpool at times, continually drawing your thoughts into a cycle of regret. But during these moments, regret is often just one step removed from nostalgia—meaning any slight nudge might tempt you to repeat past mistakes, and then, *whoosh*, down to the bottom you'll sink.

That's why God says your sins are long forgotten—erased from your past altogether. Sure, you may still notice your past mistakes rippling through your physical life, but your soul is as smooth as a tranquil pond. No longer do you have to get caught in the whirlpool of guilt—God's divine forgetfulness will give you all the strength you need to swim out.

God forgave you long ago. Have you forgiven yourself?

. . . .

*Forgiving God, thank You for forgetting my wrongs
and giving me the strength to move forward.*

FIRE EXIT

*When you are tempted, [God] will show
you a way out so that you can endure.*
1 CORINTHIANS 10:13 NLT

Imagine standing in a burning building, inhaling the
toxic fumes and feeling the heat grow closer and closer.
Suddenly you notice a fire exit to your right. You're
weak from inhaling the smoke, and this is your chance
to escape. It's now or never. Move or be consumed.

When temptation flares up like a blazing inferno,
God is not going to leave you trapped there to suffocate
and burn—He'll always make sure a fire exit is nearby.
But it's up to you to take that exit. Just standing there
and breathing smoke will only make your predicament
worse. Whenever you see a way out, don't wait until it's
too late—start running right away. God will give you the
strength to escape.

. . . .

*Thank You, God, for making a way out of temptation.
Give me the strength and wisdom to take it each time.*

IMPOSSIBLE LOVE

*Now the God Who helps you not to give up and
gives you strength will help you think so you
can please each other as Christ Jesus did.*
ROMANS 15:5 NLV

On the surface, today's command for us to show Christlike love sounds easy. But have you ever thought about what this looks like? Jesus' love for us isn't some vaguely positive emotion. It's a rock-solid, gritty determination—one that carried Him all the way to the cross. He didn't just love you—He loved you to *death*.

This kind of love sounds a bit harder to live up to, doesn't it? That's why Paul wrote that God will give us strength to fulfill this daunting task. Choosing to love isn't easy. In fact, it's often the hardest decision we face. But when we choose it anyway, following in the footsteps of our Savior, God rewards our devotion by enabling us to do the impossible.

....

*Thank You, Jesus, for Your impossible love.
Give me the strength to reflect this love
toward everyone, even those who hate me.*

WHY SO CRITICAL?

So encourage each other and build each other up, just as you are already doing.

1 THESSALONIANS 5:11 NLT

Have you ever noticed how easily criticism slides off the tongue in comparison to praise? When you hear your friends—or maybe even yourself—talking about someone behind their back, are those words positive? Are the rumors that are swirling around your school uplifting in nature?

If so, great! But if we're honest, we all know such positive scenarios are rare. Hurtful words nearly always spread faster than helpful ones—it's just an ugly truth of human nature. That's why living out today's verse requires strength. Choosing a route that runs directly against our instincts and cultural trends isn't fun, and it certainly won't score you any popularity points. But it's worthwhile because it's the right thing to do.

And who knows? You might just become the next trendsetter.

. . . .

Lord, in a world full of critics, give me the strength to lift others up instead. I want everyone to see just how loved they are by You.

CREATIVE CREATIONS

I will lift up my eyes to the mountains.
Where will my help come from? My help comes
from the Lord, Who made heaven and earth.
PSALM 121:1–2 NLV

What's the greatest human accomplishment in history? Of course, different people will give different answers, but there'll be some recurring ones too: the moon landing, the discovery of electricity, the *Mona Lisa*, and so on. Clearly, the people behind such innovations were gifted with brilliance beyond our imagination.

But who gave them this gift? Who created their minds so that they could fulfill such lofty goals? Who made the materials they could use to rise to greatness? God, of course! While the achievements of history's most gifted men and women should not be overlooked, we should never place so much value in their wisdom that we forget the one who gave it.

Humankind is truly capable of amazing things, but it's our strong and amazing God who makes us so.

. . . .

Lord, I choose You as my only source of
strength and hope—no one else.

STRANGE DELIGHT

I delight in weaknesses, in insults, in distresses,
in persecutions, in difficulties, in behalf of
Christ; for when I am weak, then I am strong.
2 CORINTHIANS 12:10 NASB

Does today's verse imply that Paul enjoyed being hurt? Not quite. Though it does mean he was able to endure suffering with joy in his heart because he knew the reason behind his pain.

Think of losing versus giving. Losing ten dollars is always frustrating, but what about when you give ten dollars to your needy friend? For you, the loss is the same—but the purpose behind your loss suddenly makes it worthwhile.

That's the kind of delight Paul was speaking of. When you're being mistreated for your faith, don't dwell on your suffering—choose instead to dwell on the one for whom you're suffering. When God is your motivation, no sacrifice will ever be too great.

. . . .

Lord, help me find strength in weakness
by remembering the reason for it all.

ACT LIKE A MAN!

Be watchful, stand firm in the faith,
act like men, be strong.
1 CORINTHIANS 16:13 ESV

Toughen up. Stand up straight. Act like a man!

Ever heard these words before? Maybe they came from your dad during a particularly rough day, or maybe your coach yelled something like it when your team began falling behind. Either way, these words are never easy to hear, but they're often just what you need.

Physically, you may not be a man yet, but age doesn't matter when it comes to your walk with God. Your Father doesn't want you to slouch in your spiritual service—He expects you to keep moving, even when it hurts. He doesn't push you out of spite or just because He can; rather, He does it because He knows spiritual inactivity is a Christian's worst enemy.

That's why whenever weakness comes knocking, a true man chooses strength each time. So, today, act like a man!

. . . .

God, I won't settle for halfhearted devotion—I'm
all in. Help me straighten up and act like a man.

MOUNTAINTOP

The Sovereign LORD is my strength! He makes me as surefooted as a deer, able to tread upon the heights.
HABAKKUK 3:19 NLT

Choosing a life of holiness and devotion to God can be a bit like scaling a mountain: with each step, looking down becomes less and less desirable. Why? Because it only distracts you from the ever-approaching goal and fills your mind with fear. When you set your eyes on the peak, apprehension gives way to anticipation.

But to reach this point of exhilarating triumph, you must first overcome the hardest part: taking the first step. No longer content with a directionless life, you choose to start climbing, knowing the goal will be worth the struggle. Soon you'll be traipsing near the top—fearless, unafraid of the gaping chasm behind you. Because the closer you get to the summit, the closer you get to the one who gives you the strength to keep climbing.

. . . .

Thank You, God, for enabling me to draw closer to You. Help me choose dedication over directionless comfort.

LIKE AN EAGLE

They who wait for the LORD shall renew their strength; they shall mount up with wings like eagles.
ISAIAH 40:31 ESV

Choosing patience is a lot like flying.

When you became a Christian, God's ultimate plan for your life was finally set in motion like a slow, steady upward draft. It's up to you, however, to surrender to it. If you start growing impatient, trying to resist the current and do things your own way, you'll never experience the full satisfaction that comes with seeing God's will being fulfilled in your life. Rather than letting the winds of time and God's providence lift you above the clouds, you'll settle for waddling helplessly in the dirt, wanting to fly but unable to leave the ground.

God has made you to fly like an eagle, so embrace His plan for your life!

. . . .

Lord, help me never to fight against the winds of Your providence, even when I feel it's taking longer than it should.

WHEN MOUNTAINS CRUMBLE

We will not fear though the earth gives way, though the mountains be moved into the heart of the sea.

PSALM 46:2 ESV

What's a "mountain" you rely on in your life? Technology? A close friend? A family member? Whatever it is, you may feel like this source of confidence is rock solid, incapable of change. But today's verse suggests otherwise.

Life has a way of tossing our most reliable "mountains" into the sea. Maybe that smartphone falls into the lake. Maybe that friend stabs you in the back. Maybe your family member gets sick. In such distressing situations, what do you do? If your trust stops at the "mountain," then you'll be devastated beyond repair. But if you have a hope beyond the hills—extending all the way to the one who made them—then no disaster will shake your courage.

Mountains may crumble and towers may fall, but God's promises stand sure.

. . . .

God, give me the wisdom to place my trust in Your unchangeable Word.

CHOOSE HOPE

*"I have told you these things so you may have peace
in Me. In the world you will have much trouble.
But take hope! I have power over the world!"*
JOHN 16:33 NLV

God knows how hard life can be. After all, He's the one
who came to earth to die a cruel death at the hands of
those He came to save. Whenever you feel alone, for-
saken by your friends and struggling against a system
that seems bent on making you fail, God understands.

But He does more than just understand—He also
gives you a hope that allows you to look beyond today's
trials and toward a brighter tomorrow. When you feel
helpless, at the whims of fate and uncaring people, you
can still choose to be strong by focusing on Jesus, your
example and your ultimate goal.

Because God has power over the world, you can
have power over despair!

. . . .

*Lord Jesus, whenever I feel forgotten, open my eyes
to Your love and give me the strength to choose hope.*

SINNERS

For all have sinned, and come
short of the glory of God.
ROMANS 3:23 KJV

Out of all the signs of weakness in a person's heart, a lack of self-confidence is probably the most noticeable. Just as the smallest dogs often bark the loudest, the most underqualified people often brag most of their own competence.

Today's verse is a reminder that none of us deserves any of this praise—we're all sinners to the core. People who think that choosing strength means elevating their own status are sorely mistaken. Strength doesn't come from those who think they're strong but from those who know they're weak.

So, the next time you do a good deed, don't brag on yourself, but instead thank God who enables you to do it.

True strength comes from humility, so choose that today.

. . . .

Lord, teach me strength through humility,
not weakness through pride. I need Your
grace just as much as everyone else.

QUALIFIED

Now when they saw the boldness of Peter and John, and perceived that they were uneducated, common men, they were astonished. And they recognized that they had been with Jesus.

ACTS 4:13 ESV

Have you ever felt unqualified to share the gospel with your friends? If so, let today's verse boost your confidence.

Peter and John were two ordinary men with no special credentials. But they had spent time with Jesus, and that was enough! Not only were they able to win countless souls to Christ but they stood toe to toe with the religious leaders of the day, unashamed to speak the truth despite these leaders' threats.

If you know Jesus and spend time studying His Word, then don't worry about meeting certain criteria or feeling unprepared—you're already qualified to share the good news. Instead of wallowing in insecurity and fear, embrace the power that comes with knowing the greatest teacher of all!

. . . .

God, help me overcome my nervousness and tell others freely about You.

FAILED ASSASSINATION

Watch yourselves, so that you may not lose what we have worked for, but may win a full reward.
2 JOHN 8 ESV

Wanna know something the devil hates? The thought of you fulfilling God's plan for your life. Satan knows God has placed you on a path to greatness, so he'll try everything to distract you. First, he'll send people to tell you how meaningless the Christian life is. And when that doesn't work, he'll start tossing obstacles in your path—minor inconveniences that soon escalate into all-out crises. And then, if all else fails, he'll find your weakest point and strike without mercy.

But despite all of Satan's "assassination attempts" on your faith, you don't have to give in. Why? Because each temptation ultimately comes down to a choice: accept or reject. And as long as you have the willingness to keep denying Satan a victory, God will ensure you have the strength to keep going.

. . . .

Father, please give me the tools I need to keep rejecting the temptations Satan throws my way.

SHORTSIGHTED

*By faith Moses, when he had grown up, refused to
be called the son of Pharaoh's daughter, choosing
rather to endure ill-treatment with the people of
God than to enjoy the temporary pleasures of sin.*
HEBREWS 11:24-25 NASB

As Christians, we understand that Moses made the right
choice by choosing God over his Egyptian upbringing.
But how many people in today's world would look at his
story and shake their heads in disbelief? "He could've
been the next Pharaoh," they might say. "How foolish
it was to give it all away!"

Such people suffer from a severe case of
shortsightedness—the immediate future is crystal clear,
but God's grand purpose is hidden from their eyes.
These are the people who choose sin over holiness,
foolishly celebrating their false freedom. For just as the
Egyptians enslaved the Israelites, sin eventually enslaves
everyone who turns to it in the name of freedom.

Are you willing to walk Moses' path today?

. . . .

*Lord, help me be like Moses and reject
the distractions of the world.*

DANGEROUS PRAYER

*When Daniel knew that the document had been
signed, he went to his house where he had windows
in his upper chamber open toward Jerusalem. He got
down on his knees three times a day and prayed.*

DANIEL 6:10 ESV

Right before this verse, the king had signed an edict
declaring all prayer—unless it was directed toward the
king—punishable by death in a lions' den. So how did
Daniel, a devout man of God, respond? He prayed.

Obviously, nobody's going to throw you into a lions'
den for praying, but what if they cut you out of their
friend group or openly mock your faith? Will you refuse
to back down, or will you cave in and join the crowd at
the expense of your soul? God's message will always be
countercultural, so it's up to you to determine if you're
willing to swim against the current.

. . . .

*Father, whenever it comes down to a choice
between You and the world, may I always take
Daniel's route and choose You without hesitation.*

NO MATTER THE COST

*Yet what we suffer now is nothing compared
to the glory he will reveal to us later.*
ROMANS 8:18 NLT

Suffering is such a broad word. If we're talking about how it's used in the Bible, it means severe, unthinkable levels of persecution. But today, from our privileged first-world vantage point, *suffering* might mean being unfriended on social media or made fun of in class.

But no matter how you define the word, one fact remains: suffering isn't fun. When we're presented with an opportunity to lessen our pain, human nature screams for us to take it. But today's verse says that when we're suffering for Christ, our best option is always to stay the course. Why? Two reasons: (1) God is always worthy of our worship, no matter the cost; and (2) the rewards for our obedience will far outweigh our current pain.

Today, let God's promise of your future joy fill you with endurance for today's suffering.

. . . .

*Lord, I'm willing to suffer for Your sake,
no matter what form it takes.*

SUPERIORITY COMPLEX

"Do not judge, so that you will not be judged. For in the way you judge, you will be judged; and by your standard of measure, it will be measured to you."

MATTHEW 7:1–2 NASB

Fighting is in our blood. Aggression and fear of the unknown course through our veins, often surfacing whenever we encounter differing opinions on what appear to be harmless topics. We lash out, cutting our opponents with insults and hurtful accusations.

We humans are tribal creatures at our core, but God calls us to rise above our natures. Each of us has a superiority complex that must be put to death if we want to live as true servants of God.

Of course, this doesn't mean we should embrace sin. Rather, it means we must resist the urge to think we are better than another human being, no matter how flawed or different that person may be. After all, the God who made that person is the same God who made you.

. . . .

Lord, help me choose mercy over judgment, humility over self-importance.

MODERN PAGANS

*"Before Me there was no God formed,
and there will be none after Me."*

ISAIAH 43:10 NASB

You won't find many wooden statues or stone sculptures serving as idols in today's culture. Nevertheless, pagan worship is more alive today than ever. People may not worship Artemis anymore, but how often do they sing the praises of celebrities? Our culture may not have temples dedicated to obscene pagan rites, but how often is perversion celebrated with an almost religious fervor?

Just as God hasn't changed, human nature hasn't changed either. People are still looking for something to worship, and if they refuse to recognize their Creator, they'll turn to temporary pleasure and unrestrained indulgence as their source of meaning. But no matter where humanity's desperate search leads them, God is still God, and He's always calling His children to follow Him instead.

Which god/God do you serve?

. . . .

*Thank You, Lord, for offering a better way than
the world's appalling system of "worship."*

GETTING SERIOUS

If thy right eye offend thee, pluck it out,
and cast it from thee: for it is profitable for thee
that one of thy members should perish, and not
that thy whole body should be cast into hell.

MATTHEW 5:29 KJV

Before talking about today's verse, let's get two things out of the way: (1) yes, Jesus is talking specifically about lust here; and (2) no, He isn't encouraging self-mutilation.

Now that we've cleared those things up, it's time for the main point of today's verse: sin—no matter the type—should be avoided at all costs. If your friend group is causing you to loosen your morals, leave and don't go back. If a song fills you with anger or impure thoughts, rip out the earbuds. Whatever the source of your temptation, "kill it," if possible. It may take a lot of strength, but it's far easier to treat it right now than if you allow the temptation to blossom into full-blown sin.

. . . .

God, help me take holiness as seriously as You do.

SPIRITUAL TOXINS

Whatever is true, whatever is honorable, whatever is just, whatever is pure, whatever is lovely, whatever is commendable, if there is any excellence, if there is anything worthy of praise, think about these things.

PHILIPPIANS 4:8 ESV

Sometimes, it seems like all the important figures of modern culture have conspired to make this verse impossible to follow. As for all the things listed in today's verse? They may nourish your soul, but if they don't nourish wallets, then the media says you might as well forget they exist.

Because the deck seems so stacked against godly living, it can be hard to maintain a positive attitude. But thankfully, in this cynical world, God is an oasis who is always waiting for His children to come to Him for strength.

If you feel sick from years of ingesting spiritual toxins, start spending time with the cure today.

. . . .

Heavenly Father, help me focus on things that turn my thoughts to You, not on things that push me further away.

GIANTS

*Then said David to the Philistine, Thou comest to me
with a sword, and with a spear, and with a shield:
but I come to thee in the name of the LORD of hosts.*
1 SAMUEL 17:45 KJV

Sometimes spiritual weakness is more than just a lack
of strength; it's an object in and of itself—a giant whose
sole purpose is to drag you away from God. This giant's
weapons are fierce and impossible to fend off on your
own. By striking at your very soul, they don't just chip
away at your willpower but change it altogether until
you see no problem with the sin you once resisted.

But there's hope. God, the one who created you
and adopted you as His own, is constantly fighting by
your side against this formidable foe. All you must do
is choose to keep fighting, and God's power will slay
the giant.

. . . .

*Thank You, Father, for fighting the giants of
temptation and doubt. Help me never to cave
in to their strong and deceptive tactics.*

WHOSE MORALITY?

Peter and the apostles answered,
"We must obey God rather than men."

ACTS 5:29 NASB

Which set of rules would you rather obey: those given by the one who created the universe and loved you enough to save your soul, or an arbitrary collection of societal expectations that, if disobeyed, might earn you a nasty glare? The question answers itself in the asking, doesn't it?

Peter understood just how trivial man's expectations are when compared to God's. Of course, we should try to live peaceably with everyone (Romans 12:18), but when the world's definition of "good behavior" clashes with God's, it's not hard to see which path we should take. Today, don't let your friends or even the "experts" tell you what's right or wrong—choose God's perfect system of morality instead. It has worked throughout all of history, and it won't stop now.

. . . .

God, help me choose Your laws over anyone else's, even when the choice isn't easy. I'm dedicated to pleasing You—and only You.

THE CENTER PATH

*If possible, so far as it depends on
you, live peaceably with all.*

ROMANS 12:18 ESV

Just as it takes guts to stand up for what's right and oppose the system, it also takes guts to sit back down when a situation calls for peace. Standing your ground on what the Bible teaches, after all, isn't the same as fighting someone over a fashion choice or music preference. Some viewpoints are worth fighting for, while others are best left alone. And even when you do have to stand up, the Bible calls you to do it in a way that is neither spiteful nor angering.

In short, the Christian life is a balancing act of sorts—a rejection of the twin extremes of bitterness and unbridled acceptance in favor of constant moderation. This path cuts right through the world's emphasis on elevated emotion and leads straight to the truth instead.

Are you willing to take it?

. . . .

*God, help me to reject both hatred and flimsy
morality in favor of Your uncompromising love.*

JUST ONE GLANCE

*"You shall not steal, nor deal falsely,
nor lie to one another."*
LEVITICUS 19:11 NASB

Imagine this: You're in class taking the most difficult test of your life. You studied the day before but not quite as hard as you should have. Now your mind is drawing a blank. As the guesses pile up, beads of sweat start to form on your forehead. *Will I pass?* you wonder frantically.

Just then you realize the smart guy is sitting beside you, his test sheet spread out for all to see. Your eyes wander to the side, and in that moment, you remember today's verse. It takes everything you have, but your eyes slowly drift back to your own paper. Whether you'll pass or fail this test, you don't know, but there's a test that matters even more—God's test—and you just passed with flying colors.

. . . .

Lord, whenever I'm tempted to lie or cheat, remind me of Your better way and give me strength to walk in it.

GOLDEN RULE

"Do to others as you would like them to do to you."
LUKE 6:31 NLT

Out of all the commands Jesus gave, this one is perhaps the one that is quoted the most and followed the least.

This Golden Rule sounds a lot better than it feels to carry it out. We all have this small but persistent urge to bask in the glow of our own humility—without truly being humble. Everyone wants the label, but nobody wants to put in the effort to earn it.

Today, choose to settle for more than just quoting the Golden Rule. Infuse it into your everyday actions—at school, down the street, with your friends, and so on. Put yourself into the shoes of everyone you meet, and then once your mind is fully in tune with the other person's situation, ask yourself, *How would I like to be treated?*

. . . .

God, it's so easy to choose self-preservation over self-sacrifice. I need Your strength so that when I'm faced with the choice, I will always choose the latter.

A CURE FOR LEGALISM

Do nothing from selfish ambition or conceit, but in humility count others more significant than yourselves.
PHILIPPIANS 2:3 ESV

If the Golden Rule teaches us to treat others the same way we would like to be treated, then today's command teaches us to have the attitude that will lead us there.

Following the Golden Rule solely out of a sense of obligation amounts to legalism—a perverse desire to somehow prove our own righteousness to others. In other words, it's just selfishness with extra steps.

That's why today's verse is so challenging. On our own, it's impossible to cultivate an attitude of selflessness. Even though we can often change our actions rather easily, it takes the Holy Spirit to change our hearts. This doesn't just happen accidentally—we must actively seek out God's heart-changing power and continuously choose the leading of His Spirit over the tug of our sinful nature.

Has your heart transformation already begun?

Lord Jesus, make me more like You—selfless and always willing to lay down my life for others.

MASTERPIECE

*We know that God makes all things work
together for the good of those who love Him
and are chosen to be a part of His plan.*
ROMANS 8:28 NLV

When life isn't going your way—when your grades start
falling, a relationship starts crumbling, and tensions
in your friendships start rising—pessimism is often the
path of least resistance. An attitude of doom and gloom
usually fits hand in glove with bad fortune, but today's
verse calls you to try something different on for size.

Paul understood that for the child of God, there's
no such thing as bad luck—or even luck at all. Why?
Because no matter how ugly this part of your life gets,
it's just one small brushstroke on God's canvas. When
it's all said and done, all those clashing colors and out-
of-place streaks will come beautifully together to form
a masterpiece.

All you must do is keep choosing to look for the
bigger picture.

. . . .

*Father God, thank You for promising that
nothing will ever happen to me without cause.*

IT'S NOT ROCKET SCIENCE

For the wages of sin is death, but the free gift of God is eternal life through Christ Jesus our Lord.
ROMANS 6:23 NLT

If you ever have trouble choosing between sin and holiness, today's verse makes it easier: sinning earns death, but God freely gives eternal life.

One of the devil's strongest tactics involves trying to complicate this message. What starts out as a mere "Well, maybe *this* sin isn't so bad" soon devolves into an all-out sin celebration, which, in turn, leads to enslavement to one's uncontrolled lusts and passions, which, in turn, leads straight to death—both spiritual and physical. By distracting everyone from the long-term consequences and amplifying the pleasures of the moment, Satan is free to sit back and watch the world do his job for him.

The choice between sin and holiness isn't rocket science. Which side sounds best to you?

. . . .

Father, give me the wisdom to deny sin's deadly deceptions and embrace Your life-giving truth.

INVISIBLE PROMISES VS. VISIBLE LIES

*Seek ye first the kingdom of God,
and his righteousness; and all these
things shall be added unto you.*
MATTHEW 6:33 KJV

Placing our hopes in what we see is a lot easier than pursuing a world that we must accept on faith. But this life-changing faith is exactly what today's verse calls us to have.

Right now, maybe for you this faith means resisting peer pressure in favor of God's approval. But as you grow older, faith will grow more and more consequential. Decisions like selecting the woman you'll marry, the job you'll choose, the hobbies you'll pursue, and the investments you'll make will all be drastically impacted by your willingness to seek God's kingdom first.

But you don't have to make these choices alone: the longer the Holy Spirit dwells within you, the more appealing God's invisible promises will seem when compared to the world's visible lies.

. . . .

*Lord God, I want to choose Your
kingdom over everything else.*

JUST ONE MORE THING

*Make sure that your character is free from the
love of money, being content with what you
have; for He Himself has said, "I will never
desert you, nor will I ever abandon you."*

HEBREWS 13:5 NASB

Have you ever craved something you couldn't have?
Maybe you saw a friend's new smartphone and immediately became jealous. Or maybe you've just been feeling dissatisfied with the way your life has been going, and you're wanting a change.

If so, don't worry. We've all gotten caught up in the attitude of *If I could have just one more thing. . . .* But today's verse tells us what that "extra thing" is: contentment. When you add this virtue to your possessions, it doesn't matter what else you gain or lose because you'll always be satisfied. And how do you cultivate contentment? That's right: by choosing to focus on what God has given you rather than on what you lack.

. . . .

*Thank You, Lord, for giving me the
keys to true contentment.*

FREELY AND LIGHTLY

"I won't lay anything heavy or ill-fitting on you. Keep company with me and you'll learn to live freely and lightly."

MATTHEW 11:29 MSG

When it comes to following God, the hardest step is usually the first one. Choosing the right thing always seems more difficult than it is, primarily because we're looking at it through eyes of flesh instead of faith. But once we make that choice—that leap over the edge— we find that God's grace is strong enough to carry us through.

That's what Jesus meant in today's verse. Even though God expects us to live in His will, it no longer becomes a difficult or overwhelming challenge because His Spirit changes our hearts to desire the very thing we need.

Only in Jesus can you live freely and lightly. Are you keeping company with Him today?

. . . .

Jesus, thank You for making the Christian life easier to live through the help of Your Spirit. Help me trust in Your power to transform my heart rather than in my own strength to choose what's right.

A NEW LAW

*The fruit of the Spirit is love, joy, peace,
longsuffering, gentleness, goodness, faith, meekness,
temperance: against such there is no law.*

GALATIANS 5:22–23 KJV

If you want to be technical about it, there actually *is* a law against the behaviors in today's verse—the law of the flesh. But since this fleshly law was destroyed the moment you accepted Jesus, it doesn't apply to you anymore. You've crossed the border from the kingdom of sin into the kingdom of God's righteousness. You're no longer limited by the tyrannical rule of greed, lust, addiction, and selfishness—your new King is a more generous leader, handing out laws that increase your freedom rather than restricting it. Even better, while the laws of sin offer only death and pain in reward for obedience, God's rules offer eternal life and everlasting peace!

Clearly, God's kingdom is so much better than sin's dark domain—why would anyone ever want to turn back?

*Lord, may I always choose Your life-giving laws
over sin's harsh and unreasonable demands.*

SELF-FULFILLING DISGUISE

*Do not be conformed to this world, but be
transformed by the renewal of your mind.*
ROMANS 12:2 ESV

In one episode of Rod Serling's classically creepy
show *The Twilight Zone*, a dying man is about to hand
down his inheritance to his greedy heirs. But first they
must fulfill one last request: wear a series of grotesque
masks—each representing the wearer's personal vices—
to a party for one day.

But when these heirs finally take off their masks,
they discover that their faces have been irreparably
molded into the masks' hideous shapes. Not only has
their greed driven them to flaunt their worst attributes,
but it has enslaved them to their own inner demons.

Today's verse has a similar message. Rather than
succumbing to our worst impulses to find favor with
the world, we must constantly choose the transform-
ing power of God's love. In His kingdom there are no
masks—only the glorious image of Christ's perfection.

*Lord, help me choose Your renewing power
over the world's self-fulfilling disguise.*

LOVE PERSONIFIED

All that you do must be done in love.
1 CORINTHIANS 16:14 NASB

Today's command might be the most intimidating of all. Love, after all, isn't something that comes naturally most of the time. It's a constant decision—one that's often difficult to choose. But as is the case with each of God's commands, you're not alone in your quest to make love your primary motive. If you know God, then you automatically know how to love. Why? Because God *is* love (1 John 4:16).

God's Spirit dwells inside you, and the longer He stays there, the more you'll start to take on His attributes. And once you realize you have a personal relationship with love personified, today's verse doesn't sound so frightening, does it?

Today, choose strength by choosing love—by choosing God. All three are one and the same.

. . . .

Almighty God, I'm not capable of loving 24/7, but I know You are. Please enable me to do the impossible by saturating each of my actions, thoughts, and motives with Your love.

PERFECT EXAMPLE

*[Look] only at Jesus, the originator and perfecter
of the faith, who for the joy set before Him endured
the cross, despising the shame, and has sat
down at the right hand of the throne of God.*

HEBREWS 12:2 NASB

God calls us to choose strength, but He hasn't left us
without an example to follow. Jesus Christ, God in the
flesh, was just as human as you are. Yet, as today's verse
shows, He willingly endured the worst death imaginable.
Why? To save *you*.

Jesus' example, combined with the fact that He
did it all to save your soul, will give you the strength
you need whenever you feel like giving up. Instead of
despairing over the way others treat you for your faith,
you'll find not only encouragement but joy at the thought
of following in your Savior's footsteps.

. . . .

*Lord, whenever I'm afraid of the cost, remind me
of the reward. And not only that, remind me of
the cost You paid to make this reward possible.*

CAUSE AND EFFECT

If anyone has the world's goods and sees his brother in need, yet closes his heart against him, how does God's love abide in him?

1 JOHN 3:17 ESV

What's the answer to the question posed in today's verse? *It can't.*

Loving God while maintaining an attitude of greed and selfishness is like swimming across the Atlantic Ocean without getting wet—it's impossible because the first thing necessarily causes the second. It's not that you must be generous in order to prove your love for God (as legalism would teach); rather, it's because you love God that you will naturally give. It's not about checking off a list—it's a simple matter of cause and effect.

So today if you find your generosity levels running low, look within and check the love you have toward the one who has given you everything. By learning to fully love God, you'll never run short on your desire to give.

· ·

Father, fill me with love for You and, by extension, a selfless love for others.

INACTION

*Remember, it is sin to know what you
ought to do and then not do it.*
JAMES 4:17 NLT

As an example of what today's verse means, imagine that a guy is late for class and sees another student frantically trying to pick up his textbooks. In that moment, two thoughts rush through his brain: (1) *Well, the Bible doesn't say, "Thou shalt pick up thy neighbor's dropped books," so I'll just keep walking;* and (2) *but I know full well this is what God would want me to do.*

In that moment, what's his best course of action? Does he ignore his conscience while technically obeying the letter of the law? Or does he do the right thing and turn back to pick up the books? Chances are, that split-second decision will reveal far more about his character than a lifetime of strict adherence to the rules.

What do your actions—or lack thereof—say about you?

....

*Help me never focus so much on what I shouldn't
do, Lord, that I forget all the things I should.*

NO COMPARTMENTALIZING

The LORD is more pleased when we do what is right and just than when we offer him sacrifices.

PROVERBS 21:3 NLT

At first glance, today's verse seems confusing. Didn't God make a big deal about sacrifices? So why does He seem to be trivializing them here?

Because the act of sacrifice had become so commonplace that the Israelites no longer understood its meaning. It became merely another rite—a ritual to be completed rather than an attitude to be cultivated. After all, it was much easier to follow a rigid set of rules, far detached from their everyday relationships and business dealings, than to plant God's values into their lives. It was convenient obedience—basic religion in its blandest form.

Today, reject the impulse to compartmentalize your walk with God, separating it from your everyday life until it loses all meaning. No amount of legalism can compensate for true righteousness and justice!

. . . .

Lord God, I'm not satisfied with checking off a list—I want to feel Your Spirit leading me in everything I do.

CONSTANT WAR

I do not understand myself. I want to do what is right but I do not do it. Instead, I do the very thing I hate.

ROMANS 7:15 NLV

As if resisting peer pressure and the sinful expectations placed on you by your culture isn't enough, your own mind can also be a source of temptation and sin!

But don't worry—even the apostle Paul wasn't immune to this frustrating cycle of failure from time to time. His good intentions occasionally proved no match for his fleshly nature, even if said nature was growing weaker and weaker by the day.

That's why it's so important to keep choosing God's way. Your walk with Him isn't a once-and-done deal—it's a daily struggle against the past that threatens to draw you back in. But the further you progress, the more your victories will begin outnumbering your defeats.

So don't give in. Keep up the good fight!

. . . .

Father God, thank You for giving me strength day by day to fight my sinful nature.

UGLY SINS

Then David said to Nathan,
"I have sinned against the Lord."
2 SAMUEL 12:13 NLV

Today's verse comes at the end of what might be one of the ugliest stories in the Bible. David had just finished committing a cruel mixture of adultery and murder when the prophet Nathan confronted him about his heinous sins.

What makes this story so terrible isn't the nature of the sins, but the nature of the man who committed them. This was no ordinary immoral man—this was King David, the giant slayer, the man after God's own heart (1 Samuel 13:14).

But notice David's reaction to Nathan. He didn't become angry or try to justify himself. Rather, as the immensity of his sin hit him, he broke down in open confession. And it's *this* action, this choice to humble himself in the face of God's righteous judgment, that sets him apart as special in God's eyes.

. . . .

Lord, I make mistakes sometimes—it's unavoidable.
Help me always to strive for Your perfection and
humble myself before You whenever I fall short.

ENDURANCE

Being in agony he prayed more earnestly;
and his sweat became like great drops of
blood falling down to the ground.

LUKE 22:44 ESV

Today's verse is one of the first recorded cases of hematidrosis—a rare medical phenomenon in which people under excruciating levels of stress begin sweating blood.

This diagnosis makes sense because Jesus saw not only crucifixion looming in His near future but also His temporary separation from His Father (Matthew 27:46). Going through either of these would be unbearable enough—but having full knowledge of both beforehand? No mere mortal could survive the pressure.

That day the full extent of Jesus' strength was on display, but it didn't take the form of conquering His enemies or effortlessly blasting through armies; it came in the form of *endurance*—the hardest (but most important) strength of all.

. . . .

Lord Jesus, I know I'll never go through half of
what You went through. In the trials I do face,
however, give me a portion of Your strength
and determination to do what's right.

UNLIMITED POWER

When the three hundred blew the trumpets,
GOD aimed each Midianite's sword against
his companion, all over the camp.
JUDGES 7:22 MSG

There was nothing special about Gideon. He was an ordinary guy with no special skill set—and that's exactly why God chose him to defeat the Midianites. By telling Gideon to assemble a ragtag army—and then to whittle this army down to merely three hundred men—God was teaching him an important lesson about the nature of strength.

Since God is infinitely strong, Gideon's decision to obey Him meant harnessing this unlimited power. So long as he stood in God's will, Gideon quite literally could not fail.

If you ever feel too weak to fight back against the world's forces of evil, don't worry—you probably are! But God has given you a mission to simply obey. And if you're walking in that mission, nothing will be too hard for you.

. . . .

Lord God, help me always choose to obey
You—it's my only chance at victory.

"ENLIGHTENED MINDS"

*In those days...everyone did what
was right in his own eyes.*

JUDGES 17:6 ESV

Nothing to see here—just a group of enlightened people
"living their truth." Judging by our culture's morality,
the Israelites had it all figured out. With no heaven
above and no hell below, utopia was finally achieved.

Right?

Maybe, if you can just look past the random mas-
sacres (18:27), extreme acts of violence (3:22; 4:21),
depraved idol worship (17:3), gang rape (19:25), revolt-
ing violations of corpses (19:29), civil war (20:20), and,
through it all, the unmistakable refrain of God's repeated
judgment on this greedy group of sinners.

On second thought, maybe our culture isn't right
after all. Maybe submitting to God's higher law isn't
an act of weakness but rather a sign of noble inner
strength—an adhesive that holds societies together
and prevents our base human nature from roaring to
the surface.

Whose idea of strength are you embracing today?

. . . .

Father, help me to always know that Your way is best.

SPIES

I am not ashamed of the gospel of Christ.
ROMANS 1:16 KJV

Many Christians live like they're in a spy movie—sneaking around through the world, pretending to blend in while secretly harboring a belief in Jesus. But is that how God really wants us to live?

Today's verse replies with a resounding *no*.

When Paul wrote these words, he'd already faced unbelievable levels of persecution for his faith. His own friends had turned against him and conspired to snuff him out. But what was his reaction? "I am not ashamed of the gospel of Christ."

In our ever-darkening culture, will you be the spark that ignites the flame, or will you try your best to blend in, losing your own identity in the process? What you choose will affect not only your future but the future of the world.

Are you a spy or an unashamed ambassador for God?

. . . .

Lord, I don't ever want to be ashamed of Your truth. Instead of hiding it, I want to reveal it to as many people as possible!

DO IT FOR THE LORD

Whatever you do, do your work heartily,
as for the Lord and not for people.
COLOSSIANS 3:23 NASB

Have you ever done a chore so sloppily that it probably would have been better if you hadn't done it at all? Maybe your lawn mowing left wide, uneven lines across the yard. Or perhaps your act of taking out the trash streaked a trail of banana peels and rotting apple skins across the porch. How did such an easy task end up so disastrous?

Simple: because your *heart* wasn't in it.

This verse says that even the nonspiritual things we do (chores, schoolwork, and so on) are important in God's eyes because they reflect our inner character— our willingness to do what's right even when the consequences for slacking seem negligible. So today, put your all into everything you do—even the "unimportant" tasks. These small deeds may just be the true test you've been waiting for God to give.

. . . .

Lord, help me do my work heartily, not halfheartedly.

WORK

The LORD God took the man and put him in the garden of Eden to work it and keep it.
GENESIS 2:15 ESV

Being afraid of work isn't just a trivial character flaw—it's a fundamental disagreement with God's plan for our lives. As today's verse shows, work was always a part of God's will, even before humanity fell into sin. Of course, this work became a lot harder after Adam and Eve sinned, but our obligations remain the same.

In a culture that increasingly values personal freedom over responsibility, it can be easy to forget that God doesn't want us to rest on our laurels. Just as He gave Adam a garden to tend, so He has given His children a life driven by purpose and goals. It may not be easy to wake up each morning with God's work in mind, but that's exactly how He wants us to live.

What work are you doing for God today?

. . . .

Father, help me find my place in life—
the work You've called me to do.

MAKING HISTORY

"Why do you call Me, 'Lord, Lord,'
but do not do what I say?"
LUKE 6:46 NLV

The difference between saying words and meaning them is the difference between a novel and real history—one simply pours from somebody's mind, while the other results from actual events that affect reality.

Making your mouth form the word *Lord* is easy enough. Actually living under Jesus' lordship—well, that's a different story. The gap between these two outcomes can be bridged by only one thing: the state of your heart. If you refuse to take God seriously, your faith will never be anything more than words—a good story, perhaps, but entirely false. But if you make the hard choice and decide to put some effort behind your words, God will give you the strength you need to start changing things.

Does your faith stop at lip service, or is your work for God making history as we speak?

. . . .

Lord Jesus, I want to work for
You, not just talk like I do.

PLANNING WITHOUT EXECUTION

*Hard work always pays off; mere talk
puts no bread on the table.*
PROVERBS 14:23 MSG

Imagine watching the final act of a thrilling action movie in which the heroes have gathered outside the villain's lair and are now discussing their plan to blow it up. The fate of the world rests in their hands.

After hours of intense planning, they finally just disperse and go home. Soon the villain's doomsday machine activates, killing everyone on earth. The end.

Not a very satisfying conclusion, is it?

Sadly, that's exactly how some Christians treat their walk with God. They meet twice a week, discuss great strategies for defeating the enemy, and then go home and do the exact opposite. They have a fantastic plan, but they lack the willpower to put it into motion. They're long on talk but short on action, and the end result is just the same as it would be if they'd never talked at all.

....

*God, I won't settle for just knowing
the truth—I want to live it.*

GOOD REPUTATION

*In all things show yourself to be an
example of good deeds.*

TITUS 2:7 NASB

"I don't care what other people think!"

Maybe you've heard people say these words, and perhaps you've even said them yourself. But while the sentiment behind this statement can be noble, especially when you're talking about living for God despite people's opinions, today's verse reminds us that sometimes we do need to care what others think.

If you choose to follow God at all times, your reputation will become equal with your identity in Christ. But if you willfully treat some of God's commands with apathy or disdain, people will notice the hypocrisy, and it won't take long for the word to start getting out.

It's easy to pretend none of your actions matter, but God calls you to open your eyes and start living with your reputation in mind. If others can't see God's light in you, where *will* they see it?

. . . .

*Lord, may my light shine before others,
pointing them to Your holiness and truth.*

DOING WHAT YOU LOVE

*Do not love this world nor the things it offers
you, for when you love the world, you do
not have the love of the Father in you.*

1 JOHN 2:15 NLT

Does this verse teach us to walk around aloof, developing no emotional attachments to anything or anyone? Of course not! God has made this world beautiful, and He has filled it with so many things for His children to enjoy.

Rather, this verse is warning us not to value worldly pleasures over our eternal reward with God. When we begin seeking satisfaction in sinful activities, that's when we know we officially "love this world" too much. It's time then to step back and rethink our priorities before the vortex becomes too strong for us to resist.

Choosing God over the world isn't always easy, but if you truly know God, it will just be a matter of doing what you love the most.

. . . .

*Lord, I want my fullest satisfaction to be found
in Your will, not in my own shifting desires.*

NO LONGER PAR FOR THE COURSE

As obedient children, not fashioning yourselves
according to the former lusts in your ignorance. . .
1 PETER 1:14 KJV

Before someone becomes a Christian, his life of sin is understandable. After all, he doesn't have God's Spirit dwelling inside him, so why expect him to resist temptation? Disobedience is just par for the course.

But when that person invites Jesus into his heart, those "former lusts" aren't excusable anymore. No longer can he chalk his lifestyle up to ignorance or helplessness; instead, God lives inside him—so any sin he chooses to pursue suddenly becomes much more unacceptable. He is not just violating God's moral law but openly disregarding his conscience. Of course, God will forgive these sins if a person repents (just like He will every other sin), but there will still be consequences.

If you've said yes to Jesus, God has adopted you into His family. Are you living like His child today?

. . . .

Help me choose to behave in accord with my new
identity in You, Lord, not my old identity in the world.

WITH GREAT POWER. . .

"Great gifts mean great responsibilities;
greater gifts, greater responsibilities!"
LUKE 12:48 MSG

Give it up—we all know what you're thinking: "With great power comes great responsibility." Spider-Man's classic motto is one of the more potent messages to arise from a superhero flick—no doubt because its meaning comes straight from the Bible.

God has given you a unique set of gifts, and the last thing He wants you to do is ignore them or use them in ungodly ways. If you're great at socializing, use that gift to tell others about Him. If your talents lie in computer software, learn how to create programs that will benefit others and bring glory to God. The better you are at something, the less of an excuse you'll have for refusing to make the most of it.

Using your talents may take a leap of faith, but once you make that choice, God will ensure the results are worthwhile.

. . . .

God, help me discover my talents so that
I can use them in service to You.

CONFESS, DON'T SUPPRESS

Confess your faults one to another.
JAMES 5:16 KJV

Verbally owning up to our mistakes in front of another person can be one of the hardest actions God requires.

Imagine that you've said something hurtful in an argument with your friend, and you walk away feeling triumphant in your victory. Soon, however, that feeling of triumph fades, giving way to guilt. Sure, your point may have been sound, but was the insult necessary?

The next day your friend starts talking to you as if nothing ever happened, but you know he remembers. In that moment, do you simply trust time and chance to lessen the sting of your words, or do you make things right before any resentment starts to build?

Today, make it your goal to confess, not suppress. It's the only way for honest, healthy friendships to grow.

. . . .

Father, help me never to be so proud that I
refuse to admit my faults to those whom I've
wronged. I want my relationships to reflect the
honesty that exists between You and me.

CYCLE OF SIN

Those who live according to the flesh
set their minds on the things of the flesh,
but those who live according to the Spirit set
their minds on the things of the Spirit.
ROMANS 8:5 ESV

Sinful lifestyles breed sinful thoughts; and sinful thoughts breed sinful lifestyles. It's a vicious cycle—a serpent forever devouring its own tail.

But if these two things cause each other, why do they exist in the first place? That's right—it comes down to *choice.* You can choose to spend your time dwelling on a hypothetical sin, or you can listen to the Spirit and cut the thought off as soon as you notice it festering in your mind. You can choose to disobey God's command, or you can choose to resist the urge and stay holy.

God has given each of us a choice. Where have your choices taken you?

. . . .

Lord, may I always choose Your Spirit over my flesh.
I never want to get sucked into the cycle of sin.

BE THOROUGH

He said to him, " 'You shall love the Lord
your God with all your heart, and with all
your soul, and with all your mind.' "
MATTHEW 22:37 NASB

When it comes to the Christian walk, putting *most* of yourself into following God is the same as not putting yourself into it at all. Why? Because once you leave that tiny gap in your affections, it will soon overtake the rest of your soul. It's like cleansing your hands of 98 percent of a highly contagious virus—if you don't take care of that remaining 2 percent, it will make all your prior washing pointless.

So, how do you put your *all* into following God? It's simple: by making sure you understand His infinite worth compared to the world's temporary pleasures. And the only way to gain that understanding is to spend time with Him in prayer and by reading His Word.

Are you all in?

. . . .

Lord, when it comes to ridding myself of sin, help me
choose thoroughness over halfhearted devotion.

EASY VS. RIGHT

What does the Lord require of you but
to do justice, and to love kindness, and
to walk humbly with your God?

MICAH 6:8 ESV

If today's verse shows us how a Christian should live, it's not hard to see what qualities we should avoid. The opposite of justice? Double standards. Of kindness? Cruelty. Humility? Pride.

Clearly, God hates these three sins, so why do we often feel the urge to harshly belittle imperfect people out of a sense of self-superiority while refusing to look within at our own flaws? Are we striving for some sort of unholy trifecta? Since arrogance and hypocrisy are far easier to achieve than holiness, it's sometimes tempting for us to choose them instead, not realizing that self-righteousness is worse in God's eyes than flat-out unrighteousness (Matthew 21:31).

God doesn't want us to take the easy way but rather the *right* way. Which way will you take today?

* *

Lord, teach me to deal justly and kindly with
others while living in humble obedience to You.

FOOLISH WISDOM

Has God not made foolish the wisdom of the world?
1 CORINTHIANS 1:20 NASB

Can you guess how much of the universe our telescopes have explored?

About four percent. That's right, given all we know about the cosmos (and it's certainly a lot!), 96 percent of it remains a mystery. If you want to go even further, scientists still don't know the secrets of quantum mechanics. We don't know how consciousness works. We don't know what lies at the center of a black hole. And as astounding as it may seem, philosophers can't even agree on what time is!

In our limited understanding, it's easy for us to convince ourselves that we have it all figured out. But anyone who truly grasps God's infinite wisdom knows that true strength lies not in knowing but in confessing what we don't know.

And as long as we're on this earth, that's a lot of confession!

. . . .

Lord, Your wisdom is far above mine.

INFERNAL PRIDE

[Eve] saw that the tree was beautiful
and its fruit looked delicious, and she
wanted the wisdom it would give her.

GENESIS 3:6 NLT

If you think about it, nearly all sin can be boiled down to one negative mindset: pride. In this verse, Eve saw the delicious fruit and decided her satisfaction was more important than God's command. She craved the forbidden knowledge—the godlike status—it would bring. She assumed that God was holding back from her something she deserved.

And so she ate the fruit.

It makes sense that pride lies at the root of humanity's sin. Not only did it drive Eve as she bit into the fruit; it also drove Satan as he tried in vain to overthrow God's throne. It was only natural, therefore, that this sin would be what Lucifer would use to introduce death into God's fledgling creation.

Today, reject the allure of pride and embrace God's humility and grace instead.

. . . .

Father, fill me with a desire to obey You rather
than to embrace the devil's oldest trick.

PRICELESS GRACE

You know you were not bought and made free from sin by paying gold or silver which comes to an end.

1 PETER 1:18 NLV

Take a moment to think about the source of your salvation. Does it lie in sinful pursuits? Of course not—that's the very thing from which you were saved! Is it found in your own righteousness? No, because humility is the only avenue through which grace can travel. So, if it's not your flesh or your spirit that saves you, what does?

To find the answer, you have to remove you from the equation. You were saved not by your efforts but by God's grace. Even the richest man alive—one who has spent his life pursuing fame and positive reputation—can never obtain this gift without appealing to Jesus' sacrifice.

Today, don't look to crumbling possessions to save you. Instead, find your redemption in the arms of God's mercy.

. . . .

Lord, I know I could never earn or reach Your grace. Thank You for Your grace that came to me.

THE TRUTH

Jesus saith unto him, I am the way, the truth, and the life: no man cometh unto the Father, but by me.

JOHN 14:6 KJV

Many people in today's world read this verse and recoil in disgust. "Who did this Jesus guy think He was?" they say. "Surely a good heart is all it takes for God to accept us into heaven!"

Well, if that's true, they're even more doomed than they think (Jeremiah 17:9). Not only are we all born with a flawed nature and a wicked heart, but we're incapable of changing on our own. Sure, we can hide our sin and appear righteous, but the wickedness in our hearts can't be removed without God's direct intervention.

So, the next time someone calls you hateful for simply repeating today's verse, don't feel compelled to accept the guilt. Jesus' sacrifice really is our only hope for salvation—and there's no shame in proclaiming the truth!

. . . .

Lord Jesus, I never want to be ashamed of Your life-giving love, even if the world tries calling it hate.

MERE INSTRUMENTS

Do not present your members to sin as instruments
for unrighteousness, but present. . .your members
to God as instruments for righteousness.

ROMANS 6:13 ESV

When God placed us on this earth, we arrived as immortal souls, breathed out by God and wrapped in fragile skin and bone.

As living souls, we have a unique gift among the creatures on earth: the freedom to choose. But the longer we stay on this dusty planet, surrounded by distracting sights and smells and sounds, the further our identity fades into the back of our minds. Soon we forget that our bodies are instruments and begin confusing them with our very selves. This worldly philosophy brings not liberation but enslavement to our flesh. We become trapped in servitude to the instruments that were intended to fulfill God's purpose.

Today, don't forget your purpose on this temporary earth. Don't forget your identity as an immortal servant of God. Don't forget that you have a choice.

. . . .

God, I want to present all of me—
body, mind, and soul—to You.

WHISPERING HATE

*With his mouth the godless person
destroys his neighbor.*

PROVERBS 11:9 NASB

You probably know firsthand how damaging gossip can be. Maybe you've sat with your classmates at lunch as they trashed the reputation of the guy across the room. Maybe you've joined in on the fun, realizing later just how hurtful your words had been. Or maybe you were the guy across the room, able to make out just enough of their words to know they were spilling the secrets you'd trusted them to keep.

Gossip isn't just a funny punch line—a harmless, humorous slinging of meaningless words. Gossip hurts. Gossip inflicts irreparable damage. Gossip kills.

Even though you probably won't be able to stop gossip from happening altogether, you *can* stop part of it—the part that once spilled from your own lips. Whenever you overhear your friends dishing out the latest round of negative news, you can choose to make sure that line of gossip stops with you.

. . . .

*Lord, teach me to use my lips to proclaim
Your love, not to whisper hate.*

NOTHING COMPARES

I gave up all that inferior stuff so I could know Christ personally, experience his resurrection power, be a partner in his suffering, and go all the way with him to death itself.

PHILIPPIANS 3:10 MSG

Paul—or Saul, as he was formerly known—could have had it all. He was a prominent Pharisee rising through the ranks, gaining respect and admiration among his peers. Given enough time, his name might have found its way into the annals of Jewish history, discussed by accomplished men even today.

But to Paul that ambition quickly became "inferior stuff" compared to the power of Jesus' resurrection. Worldly fame—especially fame built on a lie—wouldn't have done him much good once he was dead.

Nothing—not fame, power, learning, or riches—compares to the power of God's grace. Fame or Christ? The decision shouldn't be hard: in fact, God has made it as clear and easy as possible. What's your decision today?

. . . .

Lord, I choose Your approval over worldly recognition. It's the only thing that will last forever and bring true satisfaction.

TEAM GOD

Now is the judgment of this world: now shall the prince of this world be cast out.

JOHN 12:31 KJV

While here on earth, we have a choice between following God, the Maker of the world, or following Satan, the one who currently serves as its prince. It can be hard to cling to our belief in someone who hasn't yet shown His ultimate power, but we have enough evidence from the Bible and from Jesus' death and resurrection to know that this day is coming.

On that day, all of Satan's mighty fortresses will be nothing more than castles made of sand, dissolving in the flood of God's judgment. Everyone who runs to them for shelter will be exposed and humiliated.

If that sounds fine with you, you're free to choose. But doesn't a final victory sound much better than ultimate defeat? If so, choose Team God today!

. . . .

Lord, I choose to remain on Your team, no matter how strong the enemy's defenses may appear at the moment.

THE PRICE OF A SOUL

*"For what does a man have if he gets all
the world and loses his own soul?"*

MATTHEW 16:26 NLV

Today's verse gives a proper perspective on what matters the most.

When you're tempted to cheat on that test, ask yourself, *Is a passing grade really worth giving up my integrity?* When your friends pressure you to try drugs or offer you alcohol, ask yourself, *Is appeasing other people worth sacrificing my spiritual and physical well-being?* When you feel abandoned and alone because nobody understands your faith and you're tempted to give up and give in, ask yourself, *Is popularity worth more than my soul?*

When you put it like that, the act of endurance becomes a lot easier! It will still be hard at times, but the difference will be that now you'll have something to fight for.

How much do you value your soul?

. . . .

*God, thank You for this much-needed perspective.
Help me value my soul above all else in this life.*

SHIFTING SANDS

"You must not follow the crowd in doing wrong."
Exodus 23:2 NLT

The attitude that today's verse warns against goes by many names: the fear of missing out, jumping on the bandwagon, getting with the times, and so on. Often, these are euphemisms for the act of selling your soul for popularity.

When you feel you're the only person in your class doing the right thing, does that automatically mean it's no longer right? What if the worst dictator in history—say, Hitler, for instance—had conquered the world and brainwashed everyone into his sick ideology? Would his twisted morality suddenly become correct? Of course not! Conforming your morality to a morally bankrupt culture is about as wise as trying to change the laws of mathematics to match the answers given by your incorrect classmates on that math test.

God's truth will always be unchangeable, no matter how many people accept or deny it.

. . . .

Lord, give me the strength to stand above
culture's shifting opinions, clinging to
You as the bedrock of my morality.

DUST CLOUDS

*The god of this world has blinded the minds of the
unbelievers, to keep them from seeing the light of the
gospel of the glory of Christ, who is the image of God.*
2 CORINTHIANS 4:4 ESV

How does the devil go about blinding you to the truth?
By kicking the sands of doubt, distractions, and despair
in your face until you're forced to close your eyes. Then,
once you're completely blind, the devil tries his best to
imitate God's voice by tossing around words like "love"
and "freedom"—all while leading you directly into a pit.

But you don't have to deal with Satan's sand-kicking
any longer. The helmet of salvation comes with a useful
visor that, if you choose to keep it down, blocks the
deadly grains that swirl around your head. As long as
you choose to find protection in the light of God's truth,
Satan's feeble dust clouds will be hopelessly useless.

*Lord God, teach me to use the truths of
Your grace to filter out Satan's lies.*

SHADOWS

*Put away all malice and all deceit and
hypocrisy and envy and all slander.*
1 PETER 2:1 ESV

Today's verse isn't an exhaustive list of sins, but it does
a pretty good job of summing up the basics of our fallen
human nature. It's in our blood to argue and lie and envy
and gossip, all while accusingly pointing our fingers at
those whose sin is "worse than" ours.

That's why the Holy Spirit lives inside us—to elevate
us above our brokenness. We were made to serve a holy
God, but the only way we can do so is to choose a life of
holiness—bucking sin's power in favor of supernatural
sanctification. All the attributes mentioned in today's
verse become no more than shadows clawing at our
heels. We can always choose to plunge back into their
darkness, but why would we? We've found our true
purpose in the light of God's righteousness.

*Lord, help me shed my sinful nature and leave
it in the dust of the past where it belongs.*

THE STRENGTH OF WEAKNESS

Then the king said to me, "What are you requesting?" So I prayed to the God of heaven.
NEHEMIAH 2:4 ESV

As Nehemiah prepared to ask the king for permission to rebuild Jerusalem's ruined walls, he whispered a silent plea for God to bless his request with success.

Many in today's culture would see this prayer as a weakness—a "crutch" Nehemiah used to cope in a moment of fear. But that's the difference between God's wisdom and the world's: to the world weakness means relying on someone else, but to God that definition belongs to strength—as long as that "someone" is Him.

You'll never be strong enough to solve life's toughest problems, so there's no shame in refusing to pretend you are. Anyone can cling to delusions of greatness, but it takes true strength to acknowledge one's weaknesses and ask God for help, just like Nehemiah did before the king.

. . . .

God, I freely admit that I need Your help—not just right now, but every day of my life.

BOLD WORDS

*David's anger was greatly kindled against the
man; and he said to Nathan, As the LORD liveth,
the man that hath done this thing shall surely
die. . . . And Nathan said to David, Thou art the man.*
2 SAMUEL 12:5, 7 KJV

Reading today's verses, you may wonder, *Did Nathan
have a death wish?* Approaching the king with such
direct accusation sounds like a great way to get yourself
killed in a heartbeat!

But Nathan wasn't just an unhappy citizen with a
personal grievance against the king; rather, he was God's
prophet, so any words that God placed on his heart he
was obligated to speak. If his boldness got him killed,
so be it—risking his life was in the job description.

When God calls you to stand up for the truth, will
you cower in the corner, afraid to speak out in case
others ridicule you? Or will you be like Nathan and
abandon cowardice for strength?

. . . .

*Lord, may I never be ashamed to speak
Your truth, even when it's unpopular.*

NOT A HERO

*"The Pharisee. . .prayed. . . 'I thank you, God, that I am
not like other people—cheaters, sinners, adulterers.
I'm certainly not like that tax collector!'. . . But the
tax collector. . .beat his chest in sorrow, saying,
'O God, be merciful to me, for I am a sinner.' "*
LUKE 18:11, 13 NLT

Which person in today's passage do you think displayed
the greater strength—the guy who stood before God like
a hero, basking in the glow of his own righteousness, or
the guy who fell before his Maker in broken humility,
pleading for mercy?

Judging by outward appearances, we'd all choose
the first guy in a flash. But the Bible repeatedly teaches
that God doesn't care about appearances—He looks only
at the heart. And when it comes to heart strength, the
tax collector had it in spades.

When you pray, which person in this story do
you resemble?

. . . .

*Father, I'm not a hero—You are.
I'm a lowly sinner in need of Your grace.*

DELAYED RESPONSE

*Moses protested to God, "Who am I to
appear before Pharaoh? Who am I to lead
the people of Israel out of Egypt?"*
EXODUS 3:11 NLT

At first Moses wasn't the most willing participant in
God's plan. But as Jesus said in Matthew 21:28-32,
those who say they won't obey God but then change
their minds will fare a lot better than those who blurt
out their allegiance and then never follow through.
Eventually, Moses followed God right through his fear,
freeing a nation in the process.

If you feel overwhelmed by the path God has chosen
for you, don't be afraid to tell Him how you feel. Working
through your fear is a lot better than stuffing it only to
give in to it the moment it bubbles to the surface. There's
strength in honesty, especially when you're speaking
to the one who already knows.

· ·

*Father, I'm going to need a lot more than my own
strength to fulfill Your calling. Help me work through
my fear and find strength in Your presence.*

HOLD YOUR BLESSINGS LOOSELY

Abraham built the altar there, and set the wood in place. Then he tied rope around his son Isaac, and laid him upon the wood on the altar.

GENESIS 22:9 NLV

The story of Abraham and Isaac is about much more than an old man who nearly kills his son; it's a profound illustration of what it takes to give up our blessings—even the ones God has promised us—in favor of obeying Him.

Isaac was Abraham's most prized earthly possession, so by telling him to give up Isaac, God was both testing his faith and reminding him of where his priorities should lie.

What's your most prized possession? If God called you to give that up, would you be willing? When God gives you good things, it takes strength to remember not to hang on to these things more tightly than you cling to the giver.

. . . .

God, I'm thankful for Your blessings, but I hold these blessings loosely, always prepared to give them up in service for You.

BRASH OBEDIENCE

Noah did everything GOD commanded him.
GENESIS 7:5 MSG

Today's verse sounds overly simple until you think of what it really means. God had given Noah an absurd number of commands—build a huge boat in preparation for the apocalypse; round up enough animals to fill the Columbus Zoo three times over; endure the mockery of literally the entire world; and then step into the boat and watch as the rain destroyed everything. And what did Noah do? He picked up a pen and started checking these commands off, one by one.

Do you have Noah's brash obedience? Are you unafraid to drop everything in pursuit of God's will? When God calls you to jump headfirst into a place far outside your comfort zone, are you willing to take the plunge?

Today, ask God for the faith and strength to be bold like Noah. Before the rain of God's blessings and approval starts falling, you first must build an ark.

. . . .

Lord, help me be thorough in my obedience to You.

WARTIME INTEGRITY

*[Job's] wife said to him, "Are you still trying to
maintain your integrity? Curse God and die."*

JOB 2:9 NLT

Today's verse is one of the most heart wrenching in
the Bible. Satan had stripped practically everything
from Job, and the only surviving person who was close
to him—his wife—offered no other advice but to curse
God and die.

What would *you* do?

A good way to gauge what your response would
be in such an extreme circumstance is to look at how
strong your obedience is now. When your friends urge
you to do or say wrong things, do you roll over and
comply? Or do you refuse, preferring God's approval
over toxic friendships? If it's the former, what makes
you think you'd pass Job's excruciating test?

Job didn't gain his persistence overnight—it came
from a lifetime of steady obedience to God in the face
of both prosperity and pain.

. . . .

I want to have Job's tenacity, Father.
Help me build my character in peacetime
so that I'll always be prepared for war.

STAND

"Our God...is able to deliver us from the burning fiery furnace.... But if not, be it known to you, O king, that we will not serve your gods."

DANIEL 3:17–18 ESV

Talk about strength! Shadrach, Meshach, and Abednego had a simple choice: bow before the king's statue and go on peacefully with their lives or stand and get tossed into a fiery furnace.

So, they stood.

It's probable that the hearts of hundreds, perhaps thousands, of people in the crowd that day burned within them, desiring to stand but lacking the strength to do so. The king was just too intimidating. So imagine the shock those individuals felt when they heard the news: God had miraculously delivered these three men from the fire! When the next opportunity for obedience came, it's easy to imagine that these witnesses to God's power had the strength they needed to stand.

. . . .

God, help me learn from this story and stand up for Your truth, even when I'm tempted to bow like everyone else.

IS THAT ALL YOU'VE GOT?

The crowds. . .stoned Paul and dragged him out
of the city, supposing that he was dead. But. . .he
rose up and entered the city, and on the next
day he went on with Barnabas to Derbe.
ACTS 14:19–20 ESV

Pelted by stones and left for dead, Paul eventually found the strength to peel himself from the pavement. Where did he go? Did he travel home to rethink his life decisions? Nope. He said, "Is that all you've got?" and limped off to Derbe to proclaim the gospel yet again. When the world told Paul, "Stop preaching or die," Paul replied, "Now I'm going to preach even more."

Paul didn't let little things like near-death experiences stop him—he was fighting for God's eternal kingdom, and no amount of persecution could dampen the fires that burned within.

. . . .

God, may the world's persecution fill me
with renewed determination to serve You.
If the forces of evil are fighting me, that
must mean I'm doing something right!

DARK CAVES

So [Elijah] departed from there.
1 KINGS 19:19 ESV

Elijah—the mighty prophet of God who'd stood up to kings and called down fire from heaven—was now on the run from Jezebel, hiding cowardly in a cave and waiting to die. But here God appeared to Elijah, reassuring him that contrary to all appearances, he was not alone: seven thousand other faithful men of God remained.

That news was enough to give Elijah the strength he needed. Rather than staying in the cave and giving in to his weakness, he stood up, brushed himself off, and walked out. The cave had been nothing more than a refueling station—and now it was time to move on.

If you feel trapped in a cave of hesitancy or depression, don't worry. Many mighty believers have walked this road before you. But know this: God's voice will come soon enough, and it'll be up to you whether you step out or stay behind.

. . . .

Lord, may I emerge from my "cave" stronger than ever, with a renewed desire to follow You.

CULTIVATING WISDOM

"Give me an understanding heart so that I can govern your people well and know the difference between right and wrong."

1 KINGS 3:9 NLT

In the verses leading up to today's passage, Solomon found himself in a position that has been envied by nearly everyone who has ever lived. God had come to him in a dream with the words "What do you want? Ask, and I will give it to you!" (3:5 NLT). Solomon could have chosen anything—wealth, more power, good looks. . . . But out of all the visions of grandeur and unrestricted pleasures that flashed before him, what did he choose?

Wisdom.

Clearly, the seeds of wisdom were already growing in Solomon's heart for him to make this request. Otherwise God probably wouldn't have asked him. The closer Solomon drew toward God and cultivated his wisdom, the more God desired to multiply Solomon's blessings. Similarly, when we learn to crave what God wants, we'll never be unsatisfied!

. . . .

Lord, help me choose to cultivate attitudes and desires that are pleasing to You.

SUDDEN PURPOSE

[Jesus] saw James the son of Zebedee, and John his brother. . .in the ship mending their nets. And straightway he called them: and they left their father Zebedee in the ship. . .and went after him.

MARK 1:19–20 KJV

Think of how shocked James and John must have been. Up to that point, they'd lived a comfortable life of fishing with their dad. By all appearances, they weren't destined for greatness—they wished for little more than to live an ordinary, happy life that would probably be forgotten in two generations. But then came the Son of God with an outstretched hand, calling for them to change the world!

God's calling didn't stop with them—it still extends to each of His children today, even to you! So don't be afraid to step outside your comfort zone when you see His outstretched hand.

Destiny is calling. Are you willing to answer?

. . . .

Father, I want to be ready to follow You always, no matter how big the task may seem.

ENTHUSIASM

*Meanwhile, Zacchaeus stood before the Lord
and said, "I will give half my wealth to the poor,
Lord, and if I have cheated people on their taxes,
I will give them back four times as much!"*

LUKE 19:8 NLT

Few people have taken repentance as seriously as
Zacchaeus did. Not only did he turn his life 180 degrees
upon meeting Jesus, but he also decided to make res-
titution to the point of overcompensation for all the
wrongs he'd committed.

There was something about meeting the Son of
God—the embodiment of kindness and generosity—
that filled Zacchaeus with the desire to go above and
beyond what was required of him. Instead of stopping
at just following the rules, Zacchaeus displayed true
strength by choosing to obey the spiritual intensity that
now surged in his heart. He'd found the true meaning
of life. How could he ever hold back?

. . . .

*God, I'm sometimes tempted to do simply
what's required of me and nothing more.
Rekindle my love for You and help me live
by Your Spirit, not just by a set of rules.*

MIGHTY

*The angel of the LORD appeared to [Gideon] and said
to him, "The LORD is with you, O mighty man of valor."*
JUDGES 6:12 ESV

The description of Gideon in today's verse does not
match who he really was. When the angel came to him,
Gideon was a nobody from a family of nobodies, living
in the middle of nowhere.

And yet God decided to call him a "mighty man
of valor." Why? Was it because God knew Gideon had
some amazing, untapped potential? No. God described
him that way because God had chosen him. End of
story. Gideon was neither mighty nor victorious in war.
He was merely chosen by a God who was those things.

If you feel weak or helpless and start wondering if
your life has meaning, remember this: God has chosen
you for a specific task, so that automatically makes you
a "mighty teen of valor." Are you willing to live up to
the title?

. . . .

*Lord, help me live up to the reputation You've
generously given me—a title I don't deserve.*

LAST-SECOND REPENTANCE

And [the thief on the cross] said to Jesus, "Lord, remember me when You come into Your holy nation."

LUKE 23:42 NLV

We don't often notice pride in ourselves until it's too late. But fortunately enough, the second thief on the cross had the discernment to see it at the last moment of his life.

As both thieves ridiculed Jesus, one of them slowly began realizing the truth of his situation: he was guilty and Jesus was not, so what right did he have to mock? Seeing an ugly reflection of himself in the first thief, the second thief changed his tune, groaning the immortal words in today's verse. His entire life had been built on the lie that he was somehow entitled to that which wasn't his, but in a last act of strength, he admitted his own frailty and guilt.

You don't have to wait until your dying breath to surrender to Jesus—now is always the best time!

. . . .

God, fill me with praise instead of pride, helping me see the twin truths of my sin and Your love for me.

A STRONG RETURN

*I will arise and go to my father, and will say unto him,
Father, I have sinned against heaven, and before thee.*

LUKE 15:18 KJV

Have you ever felt like the prodigal son? Have you ever decided to go it alone, openly flaunting the will of your parents or even God, only to find out later that you'd made a horrible mistake? If so, you're not alone: everyone who has been a Christian for any time at all can say they've done the same thing. Our human nature is rebellious and sinful, and no matter how hard we try, it will still overtake us sometimes.

But strength isn't found in your ability to avoid sin entirely—it's found in how willing you are to accept God's forgiveness and bounce back. And in today's verse, the prodigal son chose strength.

God never wants his children to wallow in weakness—He's always waiting with open arms to welcome us back home.

. . . .

*God, help me never to stray. But if I do,
help me always to return to You.*

GENERATIONAL CURSES

*[Hezekiah] removed the pagan shrines, smashed the
sacred pillars, and cut down the Asherah poles.*

2 KINGS 18:4 NLT

Chances are, if you're reading this book, you have at
least one parent or guardian who wants to see you walk
down God's path.

But maybe you don't. Maybe a distant relative gave
you this book, and you've started your walk with God
against the current of your family's history. Maybe you
feel alone and vulnerable, like you're blazing new trails
with no map to follow.

Hezekiah certainly felt that way. His predecessor,
King Ahaz, was an extraordinarily wicked king, even
sacrificing one of his own children (16:3). But when
another one of his sons, Hezekiah, took the throne, all
of that changed. Maybe he'd been horrified at seeing
his brother burned before a pagan idol, or maybe God
had spoken to him at a young age. Either way, Hezekiah
wasn't afraid to be different no matter how many gen-
erational curses he broke along the way.

. . . .

Father, help me live as Your child, first and foremost.

CONFESSION

*[Isaiah said,] "I am doomed, for I am a sinful
man. I have filthy lips, and I live among a
people with filthy lips. Yet I have seen the
King, the LORD of Heaven's Armies."*
ISAIAH 6:5 NLT

God has a history of using the most unlikely people
to carry out His plan. A few examples: He used a murderer to free His people from slavery (Exodus 2:11-12);
a lying, swearing fisherman to be the bedrock for His
church (Matthew 26:74); a Christ-hating killer to write
a significant percentage of the New Testament (Acts
9:1); and, in this verse, a man with filthy lips to become
one of His greatest prophets.

Yet, at the same time, He also rebuked other sinners
with extreme punishments and the harshest of words.
What was the difference between them? The answer
is simple: the first category of people confessed and
humbled themselves, and the second did not.

Which side are you on today?

*Lord, I admit my flaws and weaknesses to You—
the only one who can save me from them.*

BUCKING THE TREND

*Caleb...said, "Let's go up and take
the land—now. We can do it."*
NUMBERS 13:30 MSG

Together Caleb and Joshua were the very definition of godly courage. They walked into a land of giants, looked around, and—as everyone else quaked in their boots and complained of how impossible it would be to take the land—went back to Moses and said, "Looks great! When do we start?"

Unfortunately, because majority often rules, the people listened to the other spies instead. Consequently, God punished them by making them wander aimlessly for forty years. By the end of that period, the only spies still alive to help take the land were Caleb and Joshua. Even though they'd been laughed at and ridiculed, God made sure they would receive the reward they deserved for choosing strength in a crowd of weak-minded men. Are you willing to buck the trend and serve the one who rewards the faithful?

. . . .

*God, I want to be like Joshua and Caleb—not the
ten cowardly spies who distrusted Your plan.*

GIDEON'S CHOICE

*"Take your father's bull. . .and pull down
the altar of Baal that your father has. . .
and build an altar to the LORD your God."*

JUDGES 6:25–26 ESV

Imagine growing up in a family of idol worshippers. False
gods and sacrifices have been an integral part of your
life, and your dad is even a well-respected member of
the pagan community. Suddenly God Himself gives you
a visit one night. He says, "You've been living a lie. I want
you to serve Me now. And as proof of your loyalty, you
must smash your dad's idols and build an altar to Me in
their place." Would you have the strength to obey? Or
would you choose the warm safety of familial approval
over God's righteous commands?

   Gideon obeyed. And because of his obedience, God
would later use him to free the very people Gideon had
angered with this act.

. . . .

*Lord, I want to choose Your way over the easy way.
I know that in the end, I'll never regret obeying You.*

DELUSIONAL?

"I know that my Redeemer lives, and at the last he will stand upon the earth. And after my skin has been thus destroyed, yet in my flesh I shall see God."

JOB 19:25-26 ESV

Many would say Job was delusional in today's verse. They'd use fancy terms like "coping mechanism" and "religious trauma" to explain away Job's undying faith. They'd claim that life's stress had eaten away at his rationality to the point that he searched for hope where none existed.

Of course there's just one problem with this theory: Job was right. God Himself later came to him, and just as he'd predicted, Job saw God while in the flesh (Job 40:6).

Don't let the world's condescending musings dampen your faith in God. You believe in more than just a fairy tale; and your hope reaches beyond the pain you feel right now. There's no shame in proclaiming that one day you too will see God.

. . . .

Strengthen my faith, God, when others mock it or attempt to explain it away. I know You still live!

GET BACK UP

The righteous falls seven times and rises again,
but the wicked stumble in times of calamity.

PROVERBS 24:16 ESV

Imagine you're on a long journey toward some exotic location. Your path leads you through rainforests and burning sands when suddenly the unthinkable happens: you trip and fall. Sprawled on the ground, you decide to stay there forever. No bones are broken, and your ankle is just slightly sprained; but you let the ants crawl all over you anyway, hoping some poisonous snake will come along and finish you off. There's no use in getting up. You've tripped—so now it's time to wait for death.

Pretty illogical mindset, isn't it? So why do so many Christians buy into it?

Some claim Winston Churchill said, "Success is not final, failure is not fatal: it is the courage to continue that counts." And when it comes to our walk with God, we'll always have new opportunities for courage!

. . . .

Because of You, God, my mistakes don't have to
be final. Thank You for Your amazing grace!

PERFECT STRENGTH

[Love] keeps every confidence, it believes all
things, hopes all things, endures all things.
1 CORINTHIANS 13:7 NASB

To understand this verse, let's work through some logic. The Bible says that God is not just loving—He *is* love (1 John 4:16). Therefore, the attributes described in today's verse apply to Him. And because the Bible repeatedly tells us to imitate God's love, today's verse should also apply to all of us, including you.

Therefore, you can replace the word *love* in this verse with your own name as a great way to see if you're measuring up to God's expectations. Is your faith in God steady and thorough? Do you stay hopeful when life turns sour? Are you willing to stick with the program even when you feel like giving up?

If this definition of love sounds a lot like strength, that's no accident! In God's eyes, love and true strength are one and the same, so you'll never have one without the other.

- -

Father, help me love with perfect strength.
May my strength be perfected with love.

FOOLISHNESS

The people grumbled against Moses,
saying, "What shall we drink?"
EXODUS 15:24 ESV

The positioning of today's verse makes it one of the most humorously ironic statements in the Bible. Three verses prior, the Israelites were just finishing celebrating their long-awaited deliverance from Egyptian slavery. God had parted the Red Sea down the middle and then collapsed it in on their enemies—a miracle for the ages!

And then they got thirsty and immediately forgot everything.

While we can laugh at the Israelites' foolishness from our twenty-first-century vantage point, are we really any different? When God showers us with blessings, do we remember them whenever life takes a nosedive? Do we trust that the same God who saved us once can do it again? Or do we just forget it all and collapse into a bundle of tears and frustration?

Anyone can rejoice when life is good, but it takes strength to keep trusting in God's goodness during the bad.

. . . .

Lord, may situations never determine
how I feel about Your power.

DESERT PLACES

*An angel of the Lord spoke to Philip, saying, "Get
ready and go south to the road that descends
from Jerusalem to Gaza." (This is a desert road.)*

ACTS 8:26 NASB

Imagine if all the metaphors about following God
through the desert were actually *literal*. That's the
situation in which Philip found himself in today's verse.

God didn't give Philip a road map, a strategy, or
even a clue about who he'd meet along the way. He
just told him to pack up and go to the desert. So after
grabbing some water and his best pair of sandals, Philip
set out on a mission to—well, he didn't know yet. All he
had to do was obey God, and he knew the plan would
unfold. (And it did!)

Following God won't always be easy or even sensi-
ble, but it does always pay off in the end. Because God
sees outcomes we can't even imagine, our trust in Him
will never be wasted.

. . . .

Lord, help me obey first and ask questions later.

UNSEEN HERO

When Jezebel cut off the prophets of the LORD, Obadiah took a hundred prophets and hid them by fifties in a cave and fed them with bread and water.
1 KINGS 18:4 ESV

Out of all the villainous people in the Bible, Jezebel must have been the most intimidating. She was thoroughly evil, wickedly clever, and willing to kill anyone who stood in the way of her or her husband.

But that didn't stop Obadiah. When the evil queen announced her plan to kill all of God's prophets, Obadiah devised a plan to hide them. He was the leader of an underground ring of holiness—a hundred points of light in an ever-darkening kingdom. He could have chosen the easy route and simply renounced his faith, leaving the fate of the other prophets up to chance. But instead, his heroism prevented the nation from plunging entirely into despair.

Are you willing to be an Obadiah?

. . . .

God, help me fight for the truth, even in a world overflowing with lies. This darkness is temporary; but Your light is forever.

CAIN WASN'T ABEL

When they were in the field, Cain rose up against his brother Abel and killed him.

GENESIS 4:8 ESV

Not only was Cain the first murderer—Abel was the first martyr.

Cain killed Abel because Abel's offering pleased God more. The reason behind this favor isn't given, but we can assume it had something to do with Cain's pride. Abel, however, had a pure heart before God, and he died as a result.

Chances are, your friends won't kill you for your faith. But what if they snub you for it? What if members of your own family start hating you for your devotion? And when you get older, what if you're mistreated at work or even fired for your personal beliefs?

Abel, no doubt, was grieved by his brother's anger, but the only thing that could grieve him more would have been God's displeasure. Where are your priorities today?

....

Lord, I want to be an Abel in a world full of Cains. Teach me to value You above all else.

PRIORITIES

"The one who loves his life loses it, and the one who hates his life in this world will keep it to eternal life."
JOHN 12:25 NASB

Does today's verse imply Jesus wants you to walk around in a state of depression, muttering self-deprecating statements all the time?

Of course not! Jesus wants you to have joy (John 16:24), and that's impossible if you literally hate your life. Rather, this verse uses the words *hate* and *love* to compare priorities. If you prefer your earthly life—and all the sins it contains—over God's heavenly promise, you'll end up losing both. But if you place this life on the back burner where it belongs, you'll not only gain God's approval but a life that lasts forever.

It all boils down to which lifestyle you choose—God's or the world's. The best choice is obvious—so what's your decision?

. . . .

Lord God, I appreciate the earthly blessings You've given me, but may I never value them more than the heavenly promises that await.

DOUBLE DUTY

"You cannot serve God and be enslaved to money."
MATTHEW 6:24 NLT

As a teen, you may not feel the full impact of today's verse. You probably don't have a lot of money yet, so how could you be enslaved to it?

But the word *money* isn't just the green paper you use to buy stuff—it also represents all the stuff money can buy. That new smartphone that's eating away at your social life and spiritual duties. That video game you'd rather play than going to church. None of these things are inherently bad, but they do have the potential to enslave you, driving an indestructible wedge between you and God.

The Christian life isn't a spectrum of lifestyle options; it's a true/false test. You either serve God or you serve this world—no in-betweens. Your choice is decided in your heart and evidenced by your actions.

Which master do you follow?

. . . .

Lord, I don't want to live a life of split duties. Help me have a singular purpose as I strive to please You.

WISE CHOICE

*God resisteth the proud, but giveth
grace unto the humble.*

JAMES 4:6 KJV

In a famous scene from *Indiana Jones and the Last
Crusade*, Indy and the film's villain find themselves
at the end of their quest for the Holy Grail—the cup
that Jesus supposedly used in the Last Supper. Before
them lies an ensemble of cups guarded by an ancient
knight. Whoever picks the right cup will gain eternal
youth, but a wrong pick will lead straight to death.

The greedy villain chooses the golden, jewel-
bespeckled cup, and he immediately crumbles to dust.
Indy, however, chooses another cup—a lowly, unremark-
able bowl fit for a humble carpenter—and he's correct!
The key to eternal life lay not in pride and riches but
in lowliness and humility—a poignant metaphor for the
truth in today's verse.

Will you choose wisely?

. . . .

*God, thank You for the grace you offer to those who
humble themselves before You. Teach me this humility
and help me never walk the slippery path of pride.*

HYPNOTIC RICHES

To get wisdom is much better than getting gold.
PROVERBS 16:16 NLV

It makes sense that this verse was written by Solomon—the king who asked God for wisdom rather than riches.

Many in today's world measure strength by looking at a person's wealth. In this system, the top 1 percent are the strongest. They're the millionaires and billionaires who control huge outcomes and influence their culture. They're much more powerful than the bottom-feeding lower class—pathetic creatures who are only marginally more valuable than cattle.

But God's hierarchy flips the script. In His eyes, wealth makes zero difference. In fact, large quantities of money only decrease a person's chance of finding God's kingdom. Why? Because wealth clouds perspective. It's hard to choose true strength—spiritual maturity—when the allure of worldly strength pulls on your soul.

It's okay if you never rise through the world's ranks—as long as you're following God, you're already at the top!

....

*Lord Jesus, I choose today to pursue Your
wisdom over worldly recognition.*

SEASONED WITH SILENCE

Even a fool, when he keeps silent, is considered wise.
PROVERBS 17:28 NASB

Have you ever blurted out something in the heat of an argument, only to later cringe in shame as you tried to sleep that night?

It happens to the best of us. The tongue is full of deadly poison (James 3:8), just waiting to inject any wholesome conversation with pride and foolishness. Sometimes we try filling the gaps in our knowledge with words, which end up only proving just how wide that gap really is.

So the next time you feel the urge to explode in anger or defensiveness, remember this verse. It doesn't matter how arrogant or abrasive the other side gets—you can choose to be different. Anything you say in that moment will come back to haunt you. Silence is the only way to avoid tarnishing both your thoughts and your reputation.

God, I'm ashamed of some of the things I've said.
Help me choose the stronger route next time,
seasoning my reaction with grace and silence.

RESTRAINT

*"Do you think that I cannot appeal to my
Father, and he will at once send me more
than twelve legions of angels?"*

MATTHEW 26:53 ESV

Many people try to become strong by adding action to inability. They bite off more than they can chew, attempting to reach outcomes that are entirely beyond their control. But today's verse proves that true strength is found whenever you *can* do something but choose not to.

Ability plus *in*action was Jesus' entire strategy when He was being crucified. Because He had the ability to come down from the cross and level the whole world with a single word, His inaction proved the immense power He held within His soul. He was God Himself—but He applied all His authority toward the act of restraint. This strength was what enabled Him to fulfill His plan to save the world.

. . . .

*Lord Jesus, thank You for being stronger than I
could ever imagine. Teach me to practice strength
whenever I have the power to indulge in weakness.*

WALKING IN CIRCLES

"March around the city, all your soldiers.
Circle the city once. Repeat this for six days."
JOSHUA 6:3 MSG

Which would have taken more strength—to storm the gates of a powerful city and take it by force or to walk around it in circles, trusting God to topple the walls?

The first option would require a lot of physical strength, which the people of Jericho had in spades. But God chose the second route for Joshua's army, and the strength to carry it out would have to come from within. It takes a lot of faith to stick with such a seemingly insane plan, but that's just what Joshua did. And by following this unorthodox battle strategy, he won the victory of a lifetime!

Relying on your own strength will never get you further than the gates. So today, put all your strength into trusting in God's strength—and watch the walls come crumbling down.

. . . .

Father, give me the strength to follow Your
battle plan even if it means walking in circles.

"I HAVE A MESSAGE"

Ehud said, "I have a message from God for you." And
he got up from his seat. Then Ehud. . .took the sword
from his right thigh, and thrust it into [the king's] belly.

JUDGES 3:20–21 NASB

What a message, indeed!

Israel had been oppressed by the Moabites for
eighteen years before they came to their senses and
cried out to God. And once God decides to move, not
even an evil king on his throne can stand in His way. In
this case, Ehud was His instrument of deliverance—an
efficient assassin who delivered God's judgment and
mercy with one thrust of the dagger.

The same is true for you as a Christian. The moment
you realized your need for God's forgiveness, He gifted
you with instruments of instant deliverance: His grace
and a humble spirit. Are you brave enough to give your
sinful nature a message from God?

. . . .

God, thank You for Your deliverance
that comes not through violence but
through Your mighty arm of mercy.

AUTHENTIC HOLINESS

*Prove yourselves doers of the word, and not
just hearers who deceive themselves.*

JAMES 1:22 NASB

Going to church is easy. Listening to a sermon on YouTube is even easier. Reading the Bible a few minutes each day is no sweat. But living out what you hear and read? That's when it starts to get difficult.

Today's verse, however, says this extra step is necessary for anyone who wants to walk with God. Just as hearing your parents tell you to clean your room won't make your room any tidier, merely understanding God's commands won't improve your spiritual well-being. You need to have a willingness to choose action over inaction, strength over weakness. Do any less, and you'll only be deceiving yourself. The only way to follow God's path is to live it—standing still was never an option.

. . . .

*Father God, I don't want to deceive myself into
thinking I'm holy when I'm anything but. Everyone
else can see through my outer shell, especially
You. I want to live a life of authentic holiness.*

AGREE TO DISAGREE

Determine this: not to put an obstacle or a stumbling block in a brother's or sister's way.

ROMANS 14:13 NASB

Have you ever met a fellow Christian who had a slightly different standard of morality? Maybe you were having a funny conversation and told a joke that offended this person. You've studied the Bible, and you don't see any place that seems to forbid what you said, but this person apparently does.

If so, today's verse says to respect that individual's opinion. Don't mock others or force them to participate in things they feel uncomfortable with, even if it seems okay to you. Paul knew that eating meat was not sinful, yet he refused to offend others who disagreed.

It's easy to flaunt our freedom, but it takes strength to respect the consciences of others. God wants us to live in peace, and to get there we sometimes must agree to disagree.

. . . .

God, may I never go out of my way to offend others, flaunting my opinions as fact.

TRENDING UPWARD

Turn away from evil and do good;
seek peace and pursue it.
PSALM 34:14 ESV

We're all born with a bent toward evil. At birth the trajectory of our lives is like a line trending downward to infinity, always accumulating sin and guilt yet never reaching the bottom. But when God knocks at our hearts, we're faced with a choice: accept His grace and allow Him to flip the graph upside down or refuse Him and keep taking the plunge.

Turning away from evil sounds impossible until you realize that God does all the hard work for you. You just have to choose, and that choice can sometimes be hard enough. But once you start picking God's righteousness over your own sinful nature, you'll find yourself trending *upward* to infinite goodness—God Himself.

Which equation defines your life today?

. . . .

Lord, I want my life to be a race to the
top, not a depressing plunge toward the
bottom. Teach me to turn away from my
sinful nature and pursue Your holiness.

UNHOLY WORDS

Don't use foul or abusive language. Let everything you say be good and helpful, so that your words will be an encouragement to those who hear them.
EPHESIANS 4:29 NLT

Imagine this: You're walking down the hallway toward class when someone suddenly bumps into you, causing all your textbooks and papers to spill across the floor. You're already late, so the frustration is just too much to contain. You let loose with a string of every four-letter word you know—and some you didn't even know you knew—and then catch yourself as the final profane syllable exits your lips. You look up to see that student staring at you, confused—and then you realize you're wearing a shirt with a Bible verse emblazoned on the front. You try apologizing, but the damage is done.

Don't tarnish your witness for Jesus with unholy, mean-spirited talk—be the light that matches the light you serve.

. . . .

Lord, help me choose to control my tongue, making sure no unholy words or messages escape my lips.

IN JESUS' NAME

Whatever you do in word or deed, do everything in the name of the Lord Jesus, giving thanks through Him to God the Father.

COLOSSIANS 3:17 NASB

Does this verse mean that you can do anything you want, as long as you attach the phrase "in Jesus' name" at the end? No, because that would be a direct violation of the third commandment (Exodus 20:7). Not only that, it would be an especially disgraceful example of blasphemy—using God's name in connection with sin.

Rather, this verse means your actions should always align with Jesus' will, and you should recognize His authority as you do them. It's easy to just blaze our own trails and forget the higher law we were created to follow. But when we live our lives in Jesus' name, our efforts suddenly become much more effective than they'd ever be if we were acting alone.

Whose name are you living under today?

. . . .

Lord Jesus, may my actions always conform to Your will, and may my intentions always be to please You.

LEARNING CURVE

*"Learn to do good; seek justice,
correct oppression; bring justice to the
fatherless, plead the widow's cause."*

ISAIAH 1:17 ESV

Today's verse contains a short but broad-reaching list of actions that should define a Christian's life: be fair, don't hesitate to help, and stand up for the little guy. But even though a Christian teen has the Holy Spirit inside him to help cultivate these behaviors, they don't just pop into existence all at once. They must be learned.

So how do you learn these disciplines? Simple: by sitting at the feet of the only one who has ever mastered them perfectly—Jesus. By spending time with Him in prayer and Bible study, your mindset will gradually start to conform to His. And once that happens, the choice to "do well" will become less of a struggle and more of a natural impulse.

Righteousness has a learning curve, but Jesus is the best teacher!

. . . .

*Lord, train me to be the teen You want me to be.
I'm willing to learn, no matter how long it takes.*

FLAMETHROWER

Do not be overcome by evil,
but overcome evil with good.

ROMANS 12:21 NASB

Have you ever tried to right a wrong by committing yet another wrong? Maybe you saw a bully insulting your friend, so you reacted with some hurtful words of your own. Such outbursts may feel good in the moment, but today's verse warns against them.

Fighting evil with evil is like trying to quench a fire with a flamethrower. The only way it can be put out is by dousing it with the living water of God's love. In the case of your bullied friend, try telling the offender how hurtful his words are. And if that doesn't work, talk to someone who is qualified to handle this issue.

As Christians, it's not our job to take matters into our own hands, especially when doing so would involve yet another sin. Only God's goodness can overcome human error.

. . . .

God, give me the self-control to choose Your
love, even when I feel like indulging in hate.

FORGIVENESS

"If you refuse to forgive others,
your Father will not forgive your sins."
MATTHEW 6:15 NLT

Everybody loves to hear about God's forgiveness. It's the foundation of Christianity—the driving force behind our very salvation. It's sublime in its simplicity—until we're the ones responsible for showing it.

Countless movies and books and songs and stories have been created around the theme of forgiveness. But usually they simplify the process, turning it into an emotional moment rather than portraying it as the struggle it truly is. Real forgiveness is sometimes ugly. It's a difficult, gritty process that doesn't happen overnight. It's the gradual but intentional replacement of our anger with an attitude of acceptance and love. It's our unwavering commitment to follow God's example, even when it seems impossible.

But if we're willing to choose forgiveness, God will give us the strength to carry it out. It's up to us whether we take that first step.

. . . .

May I always choose forgiveness over revenge,
Jesus, because that's what You did for me.

PLANNED OBSOLESCENCE

"Don't store up treasures here on earth, where moths eat them and rust destroys them, and where thieves break in and steal. Store your treasures in heaven, where moths and rust cannot destroy, and thieves do not break in and steal."

MATTHEW 6:19–20 NLT

Have you ever heard of "planned obsolescence"? It's a term used to describe the practice—which most modern companies embrace—of purposefully making a product to last only a limited time. That way, by the time the updated version is released, the customer is already itching for the new thing.

Well, guess what—God designed this world with planned obsolescence in mind. But He didn't do so to squeeze more money out of us; rather, He allows our lives and everything we love to break down sometimes so that we can look up and focus on the better reward—our forever home with Him.

This world is quickly growing obsolete, ready to be replaced by the final model—God's eternal kingdom.

. . . .

Father, help me choose your eternal kingdom over this broken down, faulty world.

TRUE LOVE

If I give away all I have, and if I deliver up my body
to be burned, but have not love, I gain nothing.
1 CORINTHIANS 13:3 ESV

What is love? Is it that warm feeling you have toward
your crush or girlfriend? Or is it something much more
involved—an attitude to be cultivated rather than an
emotion to be experienced?

Today's verse says it's the latter.

In fact, Paul seems to imply that love is more difficult than giving up everything you have—even your life!
Why? Because actions are just that—*actions*. Anyone
can do them for any reason, but doing them *from a
place of love* requires a close walk with love Himself
(1 John 4:8). Just as love is more than emotion without
action, it's also more than action without emotion. One
is shallow; the other is deceptive. God's love, however,
is marked by depth and sincerity—a rare treasure in a
world of plastic pleasures.

. . . .

God, help me pursue Your love, not the
parody of it that the world offers.

SINCERITY

*Anyone who wants to come to him must
believe that God exists and that he
rewards those who sincerely seek him.*

HEBREWS 11:6 NLT

God is not in the business of accepting whatever little devotion He can find. A passing interest in God isn't enough—it takes wholehearted sincerity to get His attention. Why? Because a shallow search will always yield shallow results, which will fade away as soon as life gets hard.

But when you decide to get serious in your spiritual search, something amazing happens. The truths that were once held at arm's length suddenly become as real as the ground beneath your feet. You go from simply knowing *about* God to knowing *God*. It's the difference between reading about a marathon runner and actually running a marathon yourself. Faith isn't an intellectual pursuit—it's a hands-on experience.

Are you acquainted with God, or do you have a relationship with Him?

. . . .

*Lord God, help me make a determined
push toward Your perfection.*

PRACTICAL FAITH

What use is it, my brothers and sisters, if someone
says he has faith, but he has no works?

JAMES 2:14 NASB

Many people interpret today's verse to mean that good
deeds count toward earning your salvation, but nothing
could be further from the truth.

To clear up the misunderstanding, let's rephrase
James' question: "If a guy says he just swam the length
of an Olympic-sized swimming pool, but he's not wet
in the slightest, did he actually do it?" Of course not!
It's not that the act of getting wet somehow carries you
across the pool—it's merely something that happens
whenever you try.

Similarly, our good deeds flow naturally from a heart
that's right with God. Adjusting your behavior while
neglecting your heart would be like the man in the
illustration pouring water on himself to prove his claim.

God wants more than just outward obedience—He
wants your heart.

. . . .

God, help me choose a heart change over
a behavioral shift. When the first is taken
care of, the second naturally follows.

CROSSROADS

And the LORD came and stood, calling as at other times, "Samuel! Samuel!" And Samuel said, "Speak, for your servant hears."
1 SAMUEL 3:10 ESV

It's safe to say that Samuel was probably more than a little nervous about the prospect of answering God's call. He was just a child at the time, and God's callings had been few and far between (3:1). Consequently, he didn't know what to expect; he just knew that he stood at the crossroads between two drastically different futures—which depended on His response to God.

What answer are *you* giving to God's call? Do you eagerly accept it? Or do you think, *I'm too young for this*, and expect someone else to answer? Following God isn't a lighthearted decision—it's a choice that will leave you wholly changed. But Samuel understood that the risks paled in comparison with the rewards, and so he embraced God's calling with open arms, plunging headlong into a life of service to Him.

Father, may I never turn my ear away from Your call.

GIANT SLAYER

Who is this uncircumcised Philistine, that he
should defy the armies of the living God?
1 SAMUEL 17:26 KJV

Even nearly three thousand years later, you can still
hear the righteous indignation in David's voice. Goliath
had been mocking God for days, and his blasphemous
words had recently fallen on David's ears. But even
though David was just a shepherd boy, he decided to
do what nobody else had dared: go out and kill this
giant himself.

Do we Christians have that kind of courage today?
When we hear culture mock our faith and blaspheme
God, are we quick to stand up in His defense, or do
we cower in the corner, quietly nodding our heads
while feeling kind of bad about it? Our weapons aren't
swords or slingshots—they're the truths of God's Word
and the love He has poured into our hearts.

Are you willing to stand up and use them?

. . . .

Father, when it comes to defending Your
honor, help me have the courage of David
and the grace of Jesus, Your Son.

LOOK AWAY!

David. . .was strolling on the roof of the
palace. From his vantage point on the
roof he saw a woman bathing.
2 Samuel 11:2 msg

Today's verse technically does not describe a sin. David was minding his own business, and Bathsheba was minding hers, when David's eyes suddenly fell upon an unexpected sight. In that moment, he was presented with a choice: look away or pull out a chair and enjoy the show.

He chose the latter, and at that moment David's heart was stained with sin. And because sin rarely stops at just one misstep, David soon found himself caught up in a drama of his own making. Adultery, lies, and even murder—nothing was off the table as David's flesh hijacked his rationality and led him down roads too dark for most to imagine.

Temptation is sometimes unavoidable, but the choice to look away is always entirely up to you.

God, help me never to follow David
down this path of sin. Help me to resist—
to look away and look up to You.

ASK, SEEK, KNOCK

Ask, and it shall be given you; seek, and ye shall find; knock, and it shall be opened unto you.

MATTHEW 7:7 KJV

God has given all His children a treasure trove of resources. They range from righteousness to peace, from freedom to joy, from discernment to compassion. But many Christians, for whatever reason, never choose to use these gifts—or if they do, it's only in moments of distress whenever all else has failed. Today's verse is here to remind you that God's gifts are available 24/7 to His children—no matter if your life is peacefully coasting along or barreling toward chaos.

Swallowing your pride and accepting God's offer sometimes takes strength, but in the end the rewards you'll gain by doing so will be more than worthwhile.

Ask, seek, and knock—it's that simple!

. . . .

God, I never want to go it alone, trying to live a life of holiness without Your Spirit. Teach me to ask, seek, and knock always, whether or not I think I need help.

THE RICH MAN'S FATE

*"Abraham said to [the rich man], 'Son, remember
that during your lifetime you had everything you
wanted, and Lazarus had nothing. So now he is
here being comforted, and you are in anguish.'"*

LUKE 16:25 NLT

Jesus' parable of the rich man and Lazarus is one of
the most sobering stories in the Bible. Not only does
it offer a grim warning about the fate of nonbelievers,
but it also graphically illustrates the importance of a
generous heart.

The world might look at the rich man and see nothing but wealth and happiness—but God looked at him
and saw nothing but arrogance and greed. Having large
sums of money wasn't the man's sin; rather, it was his
proud refusal to share his abundance with those who
needed it that determined his fiery doom.

Relying on the things of this world for peace will
only bring heartbreak, but honoring God—even with
your possessions—will lead to everlasting life.

. . . .

*Father, help me bless others and honor
You with all You've given me.*

NOTHING IS EVERYTHING

"Abraham said to [the rich man], 'Son, remember that during your lifetime you had everything you wanted, and Lazarus had nothing. So now he is here being comforted, and you are in anguish.'"

LUKE 16:25 NLT

Wait, you may be thinking, *I just read this verse! This was yesterday's passage!* And you'd be correct. But while we focused entirely on the rich man last time, let's focus on Lazarus today.

Most of us relate to Lazarus. We may not be as poor as he was, but we've all felt envious of the wealth of those around us, wondering why we can't be as lucky as them. But this passage shows that in God's eyes, nothing is often everything.

So, the next time you feel discouraged about your lot in life, remember that physical lack is often the precursor to unimaginable spiritual gains. Hang on—your reward is coming!

. . . .

God, help me focus on my spiritual blessings more than my physical possessions. Your blessings mean everything to me!

DON'T SHOOT THE MESSENGER

Elisha sent a messenger to [Naaman], saying,
"Go and wash in the Jordan seven times, and
your flesh will be restored to you and you will be
clean." But Naaman was furious and went away.

2 KINGS 5:10–11 NASB

Have you ever gotten furious at the truth? Maybe your parents called you out on a bad habit you'd developed, and you reacted by angrily denying the obvious. If so, your beef wasn't with the messenger but with the truth the messenger conveyed.

That's exactly how the leper Naaman reacted to Elisha's seemingly nonsensical instructions on how to be healed. Rather than trusting that Elisha's message came from God, he walked away in disbelief, thinking to himself, *What is this fool talking about? Did he honestly tell me just to take a bath?* But eventually Naaman came to his senses and made the right choice to obey and then discovered just how wise this "foolishness" really was.

. . . .

God, give me ears that are open to Your truth—
even when it seems strange or inconvenient.

LOUD AND CLEAR

*Falling to the ground, he heard a voice saying
to him, "Saul, Saul, why are you persecuting
me?" And he said, "Who are you, Lord?" And he
said, "I am Jesus, whom you are persecuting."*

ACTS 9:4–5 ESV

Saul (later known as Paul) had spent his whole life in a state of self-delusion. But in this verse, Saul found out that it's hard to ignore the truth when it's literally being thundered from the heavens!

While most of us don't have a dramatic conversion like Saul's, we all experience the tug of God's truth in our hearts. In that moment, we have a choice: (1) resist it till it goes away, or (2) start listening and letting that voice impact our behavior. Each split-second decision we make in such moments will have drastic consequences for our future, just as it did for Saul.

What's your go-to response to God's voice?

. . . .

*Lord, thank You for speaking to my soul
whenever I need advice. Give me the wisdom
to listen and the strength to obey.*

LIVE LIKE IT

Keep a good conscience so that in the thing in which you are slandered, those who disparage your good behavior in Christ will be put to shame.

1 PETER 3:16 NASB

When others mock our faith, retaliation can be tempting, especially when their mockery involves hurling untrue accusations about our character. The urge to defend our personal reputation becomes stronger than the urge to defend the reputation of the one we serve—and consequently, both are tarnished.

So, what's the best way to put your skeptics to shame? By simply living out the truth you proclaim. If you say God loves honesty, be honest. If you say God gives His children joy, don't focus on the negative. If you say you have hope, don't act hopeless.

Lifestyles are always harder to maintain than spoken philosophies. But because God's Spirit is working inside you, you can be consistent in word and deed.

Lord Jesus, thank You for adopting me as Your child. Help me live like I am Yours today.

LYING LIPS

The LORD detests lying lips, but he delights in those who tell the truth.

PROVERBS 12:22 NLT

Have you ever met someone who just couldn't be trusted? Maybe it was the popular kid in class who was always bragging about his accomplishments but never seemed to produce any evidence to back up his claims. Or maybe it was your friend who kept making promises you knew he couldn't keep.

Even human beings—whose lives are filled with cracks and character flaws—recognize a liar when they see one, and they can't stand it. How much more does God—the only perfect being in existence—detest the act of lying? Since Jesus Himself is the truth, lying is quite literally an affront to His character.

So today, whenever you feel the urge to lie—whether it's to get out of trouble, simplify a situation, or make your achievements sound better—remember that God is the truth, and the truth will always be enough to set you free.

. . . .

God, give me an honest heart.

MAINTAINING HONOR

We are careful to be honorable before
the Lord, but we also want everyone
else to see that we are honorable.

2 CORINTHIANS 8:21 NLT

"Only God can judge me."

How often have you heard those words? The sentiment behind this statement is true—God is the only one who can truly judge your heart. But *people* can also judge you, albeit in different ways.

How often have you seen a fellow Christian engaged in an activity that you saw as sinful? Chances are, it probably lowered your confidence in that person's spiritual integrity. For this reason, we should always care what people think—not to bring honor to ourselves, but to ensure God's honor isn't tarnished by our behavior.

It's easy to follow the rules like a checklist. It takes a discerning heart to make choices on a case-by-case basis, always looking for ways to bring the maximum amount of glory to God.

. . . .

Lord, may I live a life that's honorable in Your
eyes and in the eyes of all who see me.

STRAIGHT AHEAD

*Let your eyes look straight in front of you, and
keep looking at what is in front of you.*
PROVERBS 4:25 NLV

Our culture seems to be afflicted with a bad case of
spiritual ADHD. Popular perception on things like
morality, truth, and the meaning of life bounces around
like a ricocheting bullet, striking the hearts of random
demographics before moving on to the next. Not only
does this leave the world divided, but it promotes a
shallow approach to deep questions—fads in place of
foundations.

Your heart, however, is shielded by the truths in
God's Word. Even when others seem to be swinging
from atheism to New Age spirituality to agnosticism
to the occult, You can stand strong in your singularly
grounding belief: *Jesus is Lord, and I am bought with
His blood.*

In a world full of branching paths, the best road
always lies straight ahead.

. . . .

*Father, please reveal Yourself to this wandering
culture, and please guard my own heart and keep
me from going astray. My eyes are locked on You.*

LIFE OF INTEGRITY

And the LORD said to Satan, "Have you considered
my servant Job, that there is none like him on
the earth, a blameless and upright man, who
fears God and turns away from evil?"

JOB 2:3 ESV

It's possible to pull two lessons from today's verse. The first: living a life of integrity will inevitably attract God's attention and gain His approval. The second: it will also gain the devil's fury, provoking him to bring even more trials upon you.

But as we learn from Job's story, the benefits of the first far outweigh the pain of the second, even when the suffering feels unbearable in the moment. Not only were Job's blessings restored twofold, but his story was also immortalized in the pages of scripture—and he's now no doubt enjoying the eternal fruits of his earthly labor.

Integrity may be hard in the moment; but when you look at the bigger picture, the choice becomes easy!

God, help me cultivate the integrity of Job. I want
to live not for comfort but for Your approval.

JUSTICE

"Treat one another justly. Love your neighbors."
ZECHARIAH 7:9 MSG

The two statements in this verse are completely bound together. If you love your neighbors, you'll automatically treat them fairly. Why? Because true love means wanting only the best for someone, and that's hard to do whenever you're too busy mistreating that person.

"Treat one another justly" applies to every aspect of our lives, seeping down into even the tiniest cracks of our day-to-day existence. It applies to everything from playing fairly in a game of checkers to refusing to gossip about the supposedly questionable actions of that guy in your class. Justice isn't limited to elite police squads or fictional superhero leagues—it's a lifestyle choice that's driven by our love for one another. As long as there is love, there will be justice.

Is your life marked by the fruits of love?

. . . .

Father, I don't want to treat anyone in a way that I wouldn't want to be treated. Teach me how to apply my love to each of my interactions with others.

INWARD STRUGGLE

Blessed is the man that endureth temptation.

JAMES 1:12 KJV

In a haunting scene from *The Fellowship of the Ring*, a powerful character named Galadriel is tempted by the One Ring, which represents sin and greed. In this moment of temptation, her eyes turn dark and her figure is transformed into a frightening specter, symbolizing the unthinkable power that could be hers if she would only reach out her hand and take the ring. But then, just as quickly as the transformation came, it leaves, and she breathlessly says, "I passed the test."

In real life, temptation rarely looks that dramatic, but the inward struggle can feel just as intense. Today's verse, however, promises that these temptations won't last forever—their power will soon fade under the weight of a Christian's firm endurance. And in the end, God will reward this endurance with an eternal home free from the deceptive allure of sin.

Father, may each temptation function as an opportunity to exercise endurance, not to fall into sin.

COMMITMENT

*We have become partakers of Christ if we keep the
beginning of our commitment firm until the end.*

HEBREWS 3:14 NASB

Choosing to follow God is easy enough until you realize that this isn't a one-and-done choice but a lifelong journey.

If this sounds intimidating, know that the further you climb, the less difficult the road becomes. As you learn the art of obeying the Spirit, things that were once exhausting tests soon become second nature. As for now, you're still a teen, and the road ahead is probably longer than your footsteps behind. So make no mistake: things *will* get rough. You'll get tired and run out of strength, but God is always willing to offer you His own.

The righteous path might get steep at times, but the only other option is the long plunge back into sin. You've come so far—why stop now?

. . . .

*Father, thank You for the opportunity to choose
Your freedom over the sin that once enslaved me.
Keep my commitment intact as I climb toward You.*

CRITICAL MISTAKE

Though they stumble, they will never fall,
for the LORD holds them by the hand.
PSALM 37:24 NLT

Stumbling is part of learning to walk. It shouldn't be encouraged, but neither should it be seen as the end of a journey rather than the beginning.

Sin, for all its ugliness, no longer has power over your life. You're walking with God now, and as your spiritual legs strengthen and learn the rhythms of God's will, each tumble will only serve as an opportunity to learn how to walk more steadily the next time. As God's forgiveness continually erases your past, leaving a clean slate of innocence and opportunity spread out before you, failure transforms from devastating to informative.

So, what's your part in the process? To reach out for God's hand each time you trip, letting Him pull you back up to your feet.

. . . .

God, thank You for making sure my failures are
never the end. Help me learn from my mistakes, not
succumb to them. I want to keep moving forward.

UNSEEN?

*"I know your tribulation and your poverty
(but you are rich) and the slander of those
who say that they are Jews and are not, but
are a synagogue of Satan. . . . Be faithful unto
death, and I will give you the crown of life."*

REVELATION 2:9-10 ESV

In a world that values indulgence over integrity, it can be hard to keep living for what you know is true. It seems that all your efforts are going unseen—like you're playing an impossible game for an audience that exists only in your mind.

But God is always watching.

This isn't a threat—it's a reassurance. Someone *is* noticing your persistence. Someone *does* care that you're still trying to do what's right. That someone is God, and He's the only spectator who matters.

So today, don't live for the crowd—live instead for the divine audience of one. Pleasing Him is your ultimate goal.

. . . .

*God, remind me during the tough times
that You're still watching, even when it
feels like my efforts are going unseen.*

SIN-ERASING LOVE

Above all, keep loving one another earnestly,
since love covers a multitude of sins.
1 PETER 4:8 ESV

We've already learned that love is much harder than many want to believe, but this passage goes even further and explains the ultimate result of showing this kind of love: forgiveness.

When Jesus died for you on the cross, He didn't do it out of a sense of obligation; rather, He did it purely out of love for His fallen creation. Likewise, whenever someone wrongs us, we should resist the urge to hold grudges—the urge to pretend to move on while anger festers in our hearts. Instead, we should use the love that God has placed in our hearts to cultivate an attitude of forgiveness. Like oil sliding off a watery surface, so others' wrongdoings should slide off our souls, leaving nothing but our original love behind.

God's love has covered a multitude of your sins. Whose sins will you cover with yours?

. . . .

God, help me love those whom You
love—which is everyone!

IGNORANCE IS BLISS

*"God overlooks it as long as you don't know
any better—but that time is past."*
ACTS 17:30 MSG

Wouldn't it be nice to travel back to the time when innocence permeated your life so deeply that you couldn't even recognize evil? Sure, you probably said and did rude, selfish things, but everyone gave you a pass. Why? Because you didn't know any better.

Returning to that time would surely be nice, but unfortunately, it's just not possible. As we live in this fallen world, God wants us to mature spiritually and physically, learning how to separate wrong from right. The reason is simple: if we never know what good is, we'll never strive to achieve it, and therefore we'll never be able to choose God, the epitome of goodness, over the world.

Ignorance may have been bliss, but that bliss is over. Are you ready to step up and start making your choice?

. . . .

*Father, I want to live in the knowledge of truth
instead of pretending I don't know any better.*

CANCELED!

Brothers, if anyone is caught in any transgression, you who are spiritual should restore him in a spirit of gentleness.

GALATIANS 6:1 ESV

Isn't it strange how the very people who built their careers preaching tolerance and nonjudgmental love are now the driving forces behind "cancel culture"? While God-following Christians are out there loving sinners and seeking repentance for the lost like they've always done, the world has changed its tune from unbridled acceptance to punishment without mercy. Step out of line one time—even saying one mean thing in a social media post years ago—and watch the mobs descend!

Today's verse gives the remedy for the extremes of (1) love without discipline and (2) discipline without love. God calls us neither to cancel sinners nor endorse their behavior; rather, He calls us to restore them to their feet like compassionate parents teaching a child to walk.

In God's system, the only "canceling" that happens is when He cancels our sins!

. . . .

God, help me choose Your love over the world's arbitrary, changing system of morality.

SMELTING WEAPONS

*"I will remember their sins and their
lawless deeds no more."*

HEBREWS 10:17 ESV

Here's the difference between God's forgiveness and the
world's: When God forgives, He dissolves a person's past
wrongdoings, scattering their ashes to the four winds.
When people forgive, however, they often melt down
these wrongs in a show of outward reconciliation and
then spend time secretly crafting them into weapons.

Which method do you think we're meant to choose?
Certainly the second path is easier. In fact, it's often
impossible to truly forgive someone on our own. But
because God gives us His Spirit, this incredible feat is
never beyond our capabilities. We just have to choose to
forgive, and God will take over from there. The process
might take days or months or even years, but as long
as you're willing to keep trying, God is willing to keep
increasing your ability to forgive.

. . . .

*Lord, help me live free from the wrongs
of the past. Let Your love within my
heart burn away the bitterness.*

RIP IT UP!

*"Don't tear your clothing in your grief,
but tear your hearts instead."*

JOEL 2:13 NLT

A shirt is a lot easier to replace than a lifestyle.

Ripping up a shirt is a sign of momentary sorrow—an impulsive decision that may or may not be regretted later. Tearing up a lifestyle, however, takes a true change of heart—a recognition that your past life isn't worth preserving and a concentrated effort to dispose of it once and for all. Life isn't some melodramatic movie where ripping up a symbol of your sin is the same as destroying the sin itself. The credits won't roll after your decision to repent; rather, unless you have the willpower to stay the course, your sin will simply take a new form and conquer you again.

Today, don't make a show about leaving behind your past. Just leave it behind, and the resulting life change will speak for itself.

. . . .

Father, whenever I try to escape the past, it keeps mastering me. Teach me how to give it entirely to You.

BETRAYED

*[Judas] said, "What will you give me if
I deliver [Jesus] over to you?" And they
paid him thirty pieces of silver.*
MATTHEW 26:15 ESV

Experts disagree about the exact worth of these thirty pieces of silver. Some claim it was a huge amount—others claim it was little more than a week's wages. But regardless of its actual value, one thing remains certain: it wasn't worth betraying the Son of God.

Even if the value had been infinite, it still wouldn't have been enough, so why do so many people betray God for far less today? Our faith should be our first priority, but it seems that many Christians place it near the bottom. They serve God with heart and enthusiasm until the first temptation comes along and derails their dedication. Like Judas, they give up God's truth for temporary satisfaction, which then leads to eternal torment.

. . . .

*Father, I don't want to follow Judas' path.
Give me the integrity to hold on to You,
ignoring the temptations of the world.*

WHO'S THE BEST?

They started arguing over which of
them would be most famous.

LUKE 9:46 MSG

Reading about the heroic deeds of Jesus' original disciples might cause us to think of them as somehow more than human—until we get to today's verse.

You'd think that spending a few years with the Son of God would cure them of their arrogance and petty disputes, but it apparently did not. Instead, their privileged association with Jesus went straight to their heads, filling them with the one emotion Jesus was trying to teach them to leave behind: pride.

No self-exultation is allowed in God's kingdom. Why? Because none of us is more valuable than another—we're all the same in God's eyes. Because we're made in His image, we're all of infinite worth, so elevating ourselves above others is a figurative slap in the face to the one who created us. It's not just absurd— it's blasphemous.

Today, if you want to brag, brag on God!

* * *

Lord, fill me with humility and compassion,
not arrogance and envy.

STUBBORN INSISTENCE

When Pharaoh saw that relief had come, he became
stubborn. He refused to listen to Moses and Aaron.
EXODUS 8:15 NLT

Have you been so stubbornly bent on solving a problem your own way that you ended up creating a much
bigger problem? If so, you might relate to Pharaoh's
predicament (but hopefully not too much!).

Pharaoh thought that using the Hebrews as slaves
would make his kingdom more prosperous than ever.
But when God paid him a visit in the form of ten earth-
shattering plagues, Pharaoh *still* didn't get the message.
Even to the bitter end, he held on to his increasingly
absurd craving for power until finally all that was left
was a ruined, demilitarized shell of a kingdom, filled
with the corpses of dead cattle and children and the
reeking of dead frogs.

God *will* have His way, whether you obey or not. It's
up to you whether you want to simply skip to the end.

. . . .

Lord, give me the humility to bend or break my
plans whenever You reveal a better way.

BEFORE AND AFTER

*Put off your old self, which belongs
to your former manner of life and is
corrupt through deceitful desires.*
EPHESIANS 4:22 ESV

Most people have one event in their lives that separates their "past lives" from the lives they now have. For some people, it was joining a weight-loss program that brought all those before-and-after pictures to life. For others, it was a few years spent in prison.

For the Christian, this event is accepting Jesus.

But salvation is different than these other events for two reasons. First, it's an ongoing process. While those other examples might be seen as tiny red dots in the middle of a person's timeline, salvation colors the *whole* timeline red from that point onward. And second, whenever a person is saved, God snips off the timeline at that point, letting the past flutter into oblivion.

In God's eyes, there is no "before"—only "after." So why look back? There's nothing there for us!

. . . .

*Father, thank You for erasing my old self. Help me
always to choose Your new life over my old self.*

FRUITS OF THE WORLD

For all that is in the world, the lust of the flesh,
and the lust of the eyes, and the pride of life,
is not of the Father, but is of the world.

1 JOHN 2:16 KJV

Ever since Eve looked at that beautiful fruit and burned with hunger and a craving for wisdom (Genesis 3:6), humanity has shared her self-destructive impulse. All that's changed is the size, shape, and color of the tempting fruit.

For some, the fruit is green and paper thin with presidents' faces printed on the front. For others, this fruit is a tiny, glowing rectangle with forbidden images dancing on its skin. And for others, this fruit is the intangible sense of power that grows from the tree of hollow ambition.

Each day you're faced with a choice: to reach out and, at the serpent's subtle bidding, take the fruit. . . or to turn away and reach for your home with Jesus.

Choose wisely.

. . . .

Lord, I choose You over the alluring yet
unfulfilling fruits of the world.

THE MEANING OF LIFE

He finds joy in the Law of the Lord and
thinks about His Law day and night.
PSALM 1:2 NLV

Does today's verse describe you? If someone were to write a brief biography about you, would today's verse fit in context? Even more, would it be accurate? Or would it stick out like a sore thumb, unrelated to anything else that was said and with no evidence to back it up?

It doesn't matter if this hypothetical biography is filled with phrases like "strongest guy alive," "president of the United States," or "wealthiest teen in history"—if a passion for God's law is absent, what use are all these other trivial achievements? They become little more than footnotes buried in a tragedy—sad reminders of the uselessness of earthly fame.

Don't sacrifice your priceless fire for God at the altar of plastic treasures. Be bold in your zeal for Him. Be purposeful in your faith. Be relentless. Be different.

Be strong.

. . . .

God, may the words in today's verse apply
perfectly to my life. I want to be strong.

SCRIPTURE INDEX

OLD TESTAMENT

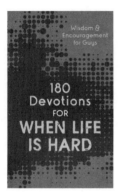